Baby
Massage

For Jason, Mimi and Jake

Also by Peter Walker

Natural Parenting (with Fiona Walker)

Baby Massage

Peter Walker

A Practical Guide to Massage and Movement
for Babies and Infants

St. Martin's Griffin
New York

Acknowledgements

My thanks to Yehudi Gordon; Brenda Hiom; Jeff Davis; Mick Smee; Caroline Holliday; Alex Watson; Lollie Stirk; Adrian Picot; Christine Jenkins; Andy Raffles; Sarah Forester; Judy Piatkus; Anne Lawrance; and all involved in the book's production. Also to all the mothers, fathers and children who modelled for the book including Lisa Climie-Somers and Seth Somers; Sara Webster, Chris McLaverty and Kieran McLaverty; Kate Daly and Eliza Daly Blanchette; Masako Kano and Maia Kano Worsnop; Uma Bhardwaj and Aroon Bhardwaj-Shah; Stephen and Olivia Budd; Sarah Parkin and Grace Lieberson; and Morag and Kimani Williams.

BABY MASSAGE: A PRACTICAL GUIDE TO MASSAGE AND MOVEMENT FOR BABIES AND INFANTS. Copyright © 1995 by Peter Walker. All rights reserved. Printed in the United States of America. No part of this book may be used or reproduced in any manner whatsoever without written permission except in the case of brief quotations embodied in critical articles or reviews. For information, address St. Martin's Press, 175 Fifth Avenue, New York, N.Y. 10010.

Designed by Jerry Goldie Graphic Design
Illustrations by Biz Hull/Artist Partners
Photography by Mick Smee

Data capture and manipulation by
Create Publishing Services Ltd., Bath

ISBN 0-312-14545-4

First published in Great Britain by
Judy Piatkus (Publishers) Ltd

10 9 8 7 6 5 4 3

Baby massage is recommended by pediatricians as therapeutic when practiced correctly. The techniques used in this book are not intended to take the place of treatment of any medical problems your child may have. Readers are advised to consult a physician or other qualified health professional regarding treatment of any health problems.

Contents

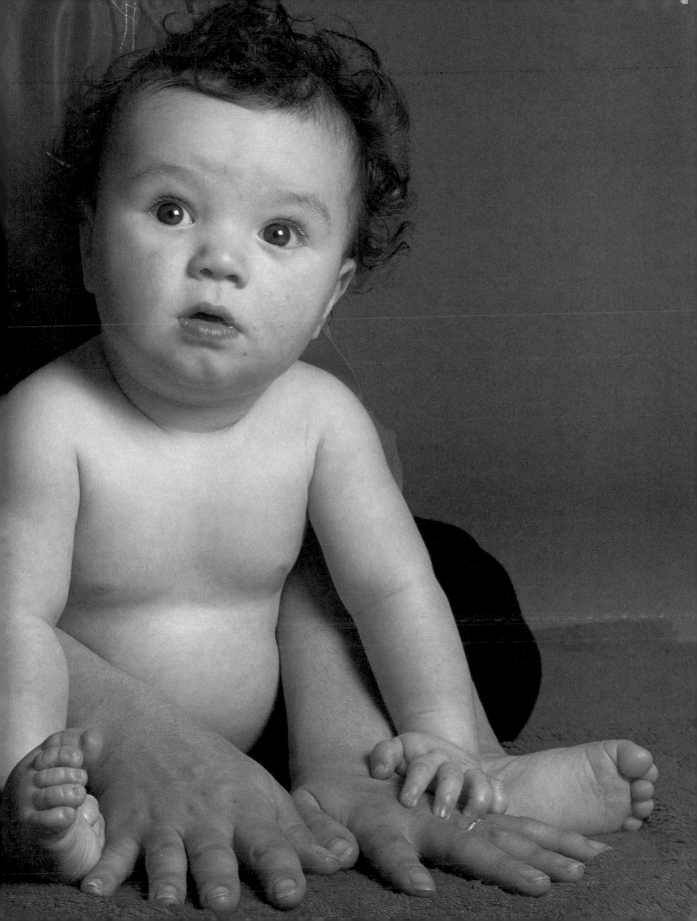

Endorsements

As the parenting of our children seems to have become ever more complicated, demanding and so open to scrutiny, it is wonderful to have a guide to our babies that encourages closeness, physical contact and stimulation, without attracting public attention. Baby massage is a way of bridging the gap between parents and children, and is to be recommended as an alternative way of encouraging a child's development, and occasional healing, without resorting to high-tech toys and treatments. As a practising paediatrician in the Western world, I see a large number of babies and parents who have 'lost touch' with each other's needs and resources. Baby massage re-establishes that contact because it may effect a cure where conventional treatment has nothing or little to offer. This book should be an essential addition to the library of any professional or parent who would like to add an extra something to their care of children.

Dr Andy Raffles FRCP, DCH, MB, BS
Consultant Paediatrician

As a mother and a paediatrician, I am convinced of the benefits of baby massage. I have enjoyed the mutual pleasure of massaging my own three children, and have recommended it to other parents. This book is written for parents who wish to provide this dimension of loving care for their children; it will give both confidence and practical guidance. It should also be of interest to professionals working with babies and infants.

Dr Christine Jenkins BSc, MRCP, DCH, DRCOG, MRCGP
Senior Clinical Medical Officer (Community Child Health)

Foreword

by Sarah Forester of

The Health Visitors' Association

I qualified as a health visitor in the late 1970s, and began work in inner London. This was a time when mothers were regularly separated from their babies at birth, when breastfeeding was controlled by the clock not by the baby's (or the mother's) needs, and when the most important preparation for a new baby consisted of buying various contraptions to keep that baby as physically separate from the parents as possible. Many of my clients, however, were African and Caribbean and as I visited them I began to learn about other methods of childcare. These families regularly used nut oil to massage their babies' skin and spent time doing passive movements on their babies' joints. Both babies and mothers appeared to gain great pleasure and comfort from these activities. Clearly, sticking with techniques that had been passed down through their cultural history, and ignoring what passed as 'expert' advice on childcare, worked very well for these families.

Since then trends in childcare have changed considerably. We are now getting back to a more child-focused approach that stresses the need for 'comfort not control' of babies. There is greater emphasis on the physical bond of mother and baby at birth, the sight of a breastfeeding mother is more common, and parents are often encouraged to sleep with their baby in their bed. It is not just the greater physical contact that has made these styles of childcare so popular. With this close physical relationship also comes a great deal of emotional contentment and wellbeing.

However, anyone who has gone through the enormous physical and emotional upheaval of having their first baby knows it is not as simple as that! The first few months after having a baby are a testing time for even the most confident parent. Many parents nowadays will have very little contact with babies until they are handed their own. And a large number of people are isolated from extended families and have to find other supportive networks. It is at this important time that many people find the support of their health visitor invaluable.

Health visitors have a 100-year history of caring for and promoting the

health of families with young children. This is a free service of specially trained nurses who visit every family following the birth of a child. Health visitors are involved in helping parents to learn the business of parenting in those early stages. This is done by both individual work with families and increasingly in the provision of postnatal support groups. It is through this work that health visitors and the Health Visitors' Association have developed an interest in baby massage.

Health visitors are discovering that baby massage provides a practical technique for helping new parents literally 'get in touch' with their babies. It helps give parents confidence in both their handling of babies and in their ability to provide comfort for their child. A baby massage session is the ideal opportunity to take a little time out from the hectic round of feeding and washing to spend time communicating with your baby through touch. Health visitors are finding that baby massage provides a great focus for a postnatal group and that individually it has enormous benefits in helping parents develop a warm and loving relationship with their baby.

Peter Walker is a well-known name in the baby massage field. It was therefore to him that we turned when setting up training days during which health visitors could learn more about the value and techniques of baby massage. These days have been a huge success and have resulted in baby massage being offered free to parents in health centres and clinics throughout the country. Peter is still involved in running days with our local centres and his commitment to baby massage as a valuable tool in the parenting process is obvious to all who have heard him speak. It is with great pleasure that I welcome his book which not only puts the case for baby massage but also provides a clear, practical guide for parents. I hope many parents will be encouraged to give baby massage a go, safe in the knowledge that these methods are tried and tested. I know that many health visitors will be happy to recommend this book to their clients.

Sarah Forester BSc RGN HV Cert Ed
Professional Officer (Education)
HEALTH VISITORS' ASSOCIATION

Left Practising backbends (see page 106).

Introduction

To develop the soothing caresses of a mother and child to a quality of touch that includes baby massage is the most wonderful skill a parent can acquire. Having witnessed first hand the evidence of this from my work as a physical therapist with hundreds of mothers and babies for well over a decade, it is my intention in this book to pass on the techniques and benefits of baby massage in the easiest and the most direct way.

Massaging your baby introduces a unique level of confidence and relaxation that is reflected in the health and nature of your child and your relationship. It is an antidote to an increasingly competitive way of life where stress plays a major part in the breakdown of human health and communication. For the babe-in-arms there is no better way, nor better time, to encourage growth and development and calm mutual anxieties and any residual trauma that may have arisen as a result of their birth or early infant experiences.

From massage to movement – sitting, crawling and walking – this book shows you when and how you can best assist your child in their efforts to achieve balance and a wide range of versatile movement. It shows you how through the even development of strength and flexibility, the yin and the yang of all movement, you can help your child to secure good posture and all the benefits that accompany it. The baby massage and soft flexibility techniques in this book originate from personal experience with my own children and from countless others that I have seen over many years. They are the ones that babies and infants enjoy the most and, being adapted to the direction of their development, will benefit from most.

Using this book

Start by reading the book through from cover to cover. Chapter One will introduce you to the importance of touch and to the background of the healing art of massage. In Chapter Two you will find the practical information needed to begin massaging your baby. A gentle routine is given for the newborn which leads into a full body routine for babies of two months onwards. Chapter Three combines massage with movement and flexibility exercises to help you assist your child through the stages of sitting, crawling and walking. In the final chapter, you will find information on using massage to help children with special needs as well as to help cope with a variety of common childhood ailments.

Once you start to massage, follow the instructions and illustrations carefully, step-by-step. Take your time, there is no need to hurry. Be consistent and with a relaxed approach practice will become easy and your touch and confidence will develop. Find the time of day or evening that suits you and your baby best and practise as often as you wish, from once a day to once a week. Persevere and the results of your efforts will become obvious.

Peter Walker
London, 1995

CHAPTER ONE

Getting in Touch

Where touching begins,
there love and humanity also begin,
within the first minutes
following birth.

ASHLEY MONTAGU PH.D
TOUCHING: THE HUMAN SIGNIFICANCE OF SKIN

Why Touch Is Important

Currently the news is that touching is no longer taboo. Contrary to what we have been told, expressing our affections within our families, and kissing, cuddling, holding and stroking our children is actually good for them and encourages them to thrive. In fact a denial of this can 'spoil' a baby by reducing their physical, emotional and intellectual potential. Babies and children need the physical assurances of a loving presence.

The only real newsworthy item in this is that we should have strayed so far away from acting upon our human instincts that this could be considered news at all. Western society has become so impersonal and desensitised to the value of loving touch that from the very first moments of birth many mothers are discouraged from expressing this, by having their babies routinely removed. Disempower any other mammal after such a momentous event, deny her the opportunity to feed or feel for her offspring, and the mother will almost certainly reject her newborn or change her mode of behaviour towards it.

The parent as carer

To console or to control your infant? To love and nurture your child or create independence through isolation and solitude? This is a Western dilemma which arose from a patriarchal, industrialised society and a conformist and mechanical method of 1920s' child psychology termed 'Behaviourism'. That these issues should even pose a question would be deemed absurd in other cultures where the baby's needs are accepted, and close physical contact follows on from birth as a natural and essential part of childcare.

Moving from Behaviourism into an era of psychological awareness, we should now know the immense value and influence that primal care has upon the health and development of the child. During the first three years while constructing coordinate patterns for physical and mental skills, babies absorb more information than at any other time in their lives. Although the importance of this goes mainly unrecognised by society at large, as a parent you are your baby's main teacher and caretaker during the most critical and formative period of their life – a period of rapid physical and emotional development.

Unlike other mammals, who are on their feet within minutes of birth and largely independent within weeks, humankind's achievements are far more complex; consequently our babies remain dependent for a longer period of time. The younger the child, the more vulnerable and greater their need for physical reassurance.

Few people would dispute the joys of nurturing a young child, but as a dependent presence they can at times demand unbelievable levels of endurance and tolerance. They also possess the unique ability of being able to make the most conscientious parent feel totally inadequate. In circumstances like this, 'to console rather than control' is far more likely to be included as an option if you know techniques or have developed the ability to do it.

Touch and communication

Touch is the most developed of the senses at birth and the prime means of communication. As such, touch is regarded as the 'mother' sense, and plays a significant role in parent and child relationships. To develop this sense, massaging your baby offers you the best possible way to get the feel of him and be able to handle him with more ease and confidence. For both parent and child the benefits of baby massage are extensive, and include a far higher degree of mutual trust with less fractiousness on the part of the child and less parental anxiety. Given at this time when it is most needed, a baby is very receptive to it. As well as the emotional benefits, regularly massaging your baby stimulates survival mechanisms such as the circulatory system (not fully developed at birth), and processes of digestion and elimination. It also encourages muscular coordination and can influence aspects of your child's development.

Father and baby

For fathers who wish to include themselves in a more active role and feature as more equal in early childcare the benefits are immense. Massaging your baby will bring you far more in touch with your child, will help improve upon your ability to cope with your child during more stressful moments, and retrieve feelings often neglected in males in favour of a more macho image.

'If you don't use it, you lose it'

After the confinement of the womb, during their first months of life when lying on their backs and their bellies, babies stretch out their bodies and create a wonderful degree of flexible movements. Once sitting and standing the emphasis then changes more from flexibility to strength. From this time on, as babies lift and carry their rapidly increasing body weight, they become weightlifters and strengthen rapidly. 'If you don't use it, you lose it' is a rule of nature, however, and like all weightlifters a degree of flexibility is lost at this time, unless it has already been firmly established and maintained. Knowing the movements that babies make or are able to make, you can ensure through playful practice that flexibility is maintained as your infant strengthens. The even development of strength and flexibility is the essence of good posture. Although helping a child to sit, stand and walk is an everyday part of childcare, the child learns in months what took humankind millions of years to develop; the importance of how you help should not be overlooked.

The combined benefits of massage and a flexible well-balanced body offer your child physical, intellectual and emotional benefits and for you it offers the best possible way to set your child on his or her own two feet at the start of the road to independence.

About Massage

As the oldest and the most natural of all the healing arts, massage has been practised to ease childbirth, aid recovery, stimulate and soothe babies and remedy a variety of adult ailments in many cultures the world over. Throughout the East and the Orient midwives massage mothers and mothers massage their babies; and from the barbers who massage their clients' heads to the traditional reflexologists who massage their clients' feet, massage is used as a customary part of daily life to heal, invigorate, and relax men and women from all walks of life.

In the West it is only comparatively recently that massage has been more publicly accepted as being beneficial, and its merits recognised by most medical practitioners. Currently baby massage is enjoying more general media and medical acknowledgements and has been introduced into many of our hospital maternity wards and special baby care units. Some members of the Royal College of Midwives are now teaching new mothers how to massage their babies, and workshops for health visitors organised by the Health Visitors' Association have encouraged their members to establish baby massage groups in local child healthcare clinics nationwide.

Massage in other cultures

The association of massage with health then is not a new one. In the first recognised medical texts – authentic ancient records of Hippocrates, the renowned Greek physician (460–377 BC) – massage is given pride of place in the physician's arts. 'The physician must be experienced in all things but assuredly rubbing' it states. Miraculous cures through the laying on of hands are recorded in some of our most ancient books and manuscripts. The Bible tells how Jesus Christ and many saints were possessed of the power to heal through the medium of a loving touch.

The first aromatherapists

From these early records we also find evidence of the great esteem given to specific resins, herbs and spices – renowned for their fragrant and healing properties – which were used in the concoctions of the apothecaries and original aromatherapists. 'Pure myrrh, sweet cinnamon, sweet calamus, cassia and olive oil ... an oil of holy ointment, an ointment compound after the art of the apothecary' (*Exodus 30*, where God gives to Moses the constituents of a sacred oil.) For the ancient Greeks oils and spices were highly valued. With an empire that stretched from the Nile to the Indus, these aromatic constituents became precious merchandise for ancient traders.

The antiseptic and healing qualities of the balms and unctions of the early aromatherapist, combined with massage and bathing, played a major role in maintaining the health of ancient cultures. Long before the realisation in eighteenth-century medicine that physicians must wash their hands to prevent the spread of disease, health and hygiene were made synonymous in ancient Greece. The word hygiene originates from the Greek *higienos*, meaning good health, and in this golden civilisation every walled village had a public bath. Like the baths of the Romans and the public baths or Hammans now established in every major town in all Islamic countries – and like our own 'Turkish vapour baths' – these were a meeting place for people to gather to bathe and be massaged.

Massage at birth

In many cultures throughout the world massage is introduced at birth. As a routine part of early childcare, societies like the Ibo of Nigeria and Kwakiatis of North America massage their newborn to stimulate their survival mechanisms and help them resist disease. As an essential skill of the traditional midwife in many other societies, mothers are massaged before and during labour, and after the birth both mother and baby are massaged daily. This varies from every day for the first twelve days in Gujarat to the first thirty days in the Punjab, and varying periods in other parts of India, Malaysia, Mexico, Thailand, Java, Tahiti, China, the Phillipines, Vietnam, Ceylon and Indonesia.

The Newborn

Your newborn baby sees, hears, tastes, smells and feels from the first moments of birth and will respond very clearly to the way in which he is handled and to the kind of stimulation received from his immediate environment. The trauma of birth, suffered to a greater or lesser degree by all babies, is soothed by the immediate physical contact that they share with their mother – the skin to skin contact, cradling, feeding, suckling and other forms of tactile sensation they receive. This period of time immediately following the baby's birth is recognised as a significant interval for attachment in the mother and child relationship. For fathers given the opportunity to be present or take part in the birth, this kind of relationship can also be established, by holding, stroking and soothing their newborn. In the event of the mother needing rest or medical attention, it could well be the father who first spends time with the baby, but with either or both parents, the baby is known to respond equally well.

Although the natural conditions set for parent and child attachment and bonding are most favourable in the time immediately following birth, should circumstances make this impossible – for example if you adopt your baby, if the father cannot be present, or your baby needs special care – observation has shown that this kind of bond can still be established later on.

From the womb to the world

For the baby, the transition from the haven of the womb to the external world entails a major adjustment. Since the beginning of time the baby has been conditioned by the warmth of the mother, used to the constant embrace of her womb and has been nurtured, nourished and protected without having to make any demands. From the omnipotence of the womb, a recipient of continual, unconditional care at one with their environment, the babe-in-arms is now a separate entity and must adjust to a time interval between recognising her needs and having them fulfilled. The period of time it takes for the child to understand that she is separate is known to be an emotionally difficult one, and it is not for some two years that children have a really clear idea of themselves as individuals. Throughout this time and in varying degrees thereafter, babies are likely to experience extreme emotions when they cannot get what they need or want, precisely when they need or want it.

During the early months an 'in-arms' or period of close physical contact seems to provide a continuity of the kind of experience that the baby has been conditioned to in the womb, and makes the fulfilment of her needs and adjustment to her new environment easier. The 'in-arms' period is a transitional one, which will allow the child to literally 'gather her senses' in a new and unfamiliar world. This period of emotional adjustment and consolidation of the senses is facilitated by close physical contact. Babies respond well to being carried and rocked, because it is one of the few things that is familiar – the sense of kinesthesia, or body in motion, having already been developed by these same movements in utero. Similarly, babies respond well to being stroked because the area of the brain's cortex that processes this sense is more developed at birth than any other area.

Identifying the parent

During the first two or three months the recognition of the parent or main caretaker takes place on the basis of sound and smell. Focused vision is also present, but is restricted from about eight to twelve inches and it is no coincidence that this is the distance between the breast or hand that feeds the baby and the mother or father's face. Within days of birth the baby will turn towards the smell of his mother's breast, and show more preference for her smell and taste than any other. Our sense of smell is thought to be closely related to early memory and for many adults a particular smell can arouse the nostalgia of early infancy and the memory of a particularly pleasant experience. It is also not unusual for an infant to retain an item of clothing or bed linen from which he will obtain great comfort from smelling. Not all smells are pleasant however and for some babies an acrid aroma such as tobacco, some brands of furniture polish, disinfectants, air fresheners,

Right The young baby can focus as far as his mother's face whilst feeding.

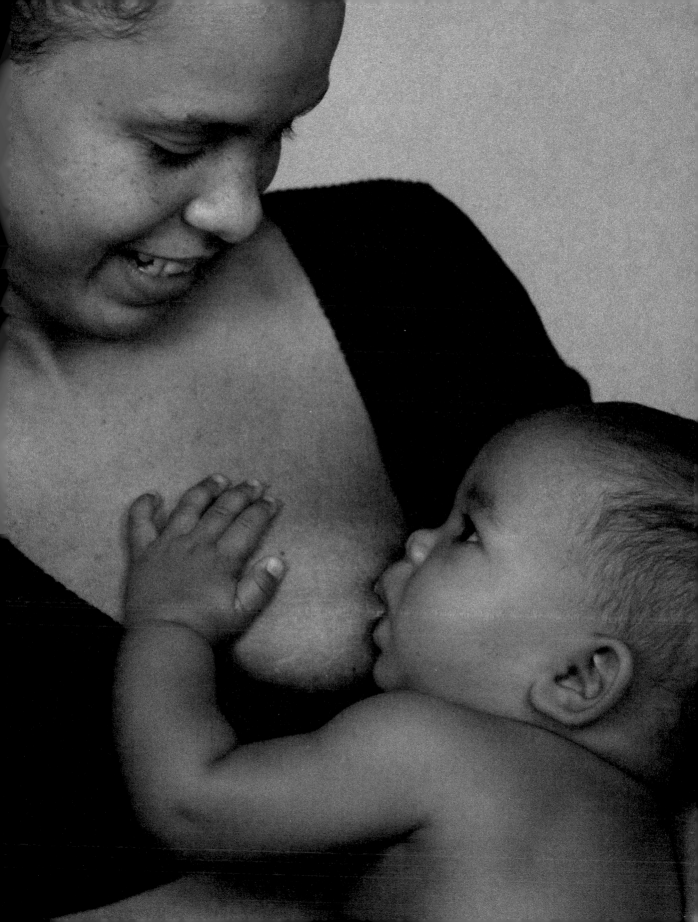

perfumes and aftershaves could account for some inexplicable episodes of crying.

The baby's senses of sound, sight, touch, taste and smell develop and coordinate with close physical contact and his interaction with his immediate environment. Some of the baby's earliest perceptions are organised around suckling, and hand and finger movements around the mother's breast. During these early months, the baby's reflex activities like 'walking', 'rooting', 'grasping', 'sucking', and 'reaching out' will be lost, or consolidated and strengthened through use they then become voluntary or willed movements.

The eyes, ears, nose, mouth and hands are the tools of intelligence, and the first step towards intelligent behaviour is the development and coordination of their abilities. What is learned through explorative activities around the mother forms the basis for further learning, like joint explorations of the hand to the mouth, then visual coordinations with hand to mouth, and so forth.

We can see therefore that emotional, psychological and physical development is nourished by the attachment that the baby forms with another human being. The continuity of physical warmth provided by an 'in-arms' period fosters the confidence needed for gradual separation and independence. And, as well as the organisation of the senses, an 'in-arms' period also encourages strength and coordination in the muscles that support the head, neck and spine when held upright.

Touch and early development

The benefits of a period of close physical contact is supported by research from many parts of the world. In his book *Touching*, aside from his own detailed observations, Dr Ashley Montagu includes those of anthropologists such as Margaret Mead on Balinese children and the Arapesh in New Guinea, Richard James de Boer on the Netsilik eskimos, Dr Patricia Draper on the bushmen of the Kalahari, and Dr Mary Ainsworth and Marcelle Geber on the Ganda children of East Africa. From these and many other third world studies in which babies are cradled, sung to, stroked, caressed and carried by their mothers and other family members, their overall development is noted as remarkably well advanced.

Jean Liedloff, in her book *The Continuum Concept*, describes her experiences living with the Yequana Indians of South America for some two-and-a-half years. Liedloff refers to the innate ability 'that is awakened in us all in response to the vulnerability of a baby', the maternal and paternal instincts which, if they have not been fractured by our own childhood experiences, impel us to respond adequately to the baby's emotional needs. For the Yequana Indians, childhood begins with a period of close physical contact, an 'in-arms' period up to crawling, which Liedloff and others have confirmed as having a profound effect upon the growth and personality of the child and the adult.

Adult behaviour and personality characteristics are shaped by the events of infancy and childhood. The baby's whole body responds with emotion, with every feeling there is a muscular impression. These impressions accrue from the core, and are visible in the postures and movements of early childhood. Happy children are confident, resilient and optimistic, and their emotional state is directly reflected in their physical being – upright, open, free and relaxed. Fulfilling the tactile needs of the baby is the first step towards maintaining the concepts instilled in the womb of a benevolent and caring world amply provided to meet the child's needs.

The infant's need for body contact is compelling. If that need is not adequately satisfied, even though all other needs are adequately met, he or she will suffer.

Dr Ashley Montagu
Touching: The Human Significance of Skin

Overleaf Massage brings fathers more in touch
with their new baby.

If you cannot, through social or economic circumstances, maintain a relationship of this nature with your child, predictable repeated separations – where well-chosen alternative care arrangements are provided, especially an 'in-arms' alternative – need not necessarily reduce the quality of your relationship with your child. While consistent child/parent contact is preferable, the quality of contact under these circumstances can do much towards compensating for the quantity.

Developing the language of touch

When we use expressions like: 'to have the feel of', 'to be in touch with', 'to be able to handle', we describe human relationships in terms of our sense of touch. At no other time of life is this more true than with your young baby. As we now know, the way in which babies are touched and held, and the frequency with which this is done, has a marked effect. Cuddly toys and woolly blankets may have their uses, but they make poor substitutes for the warmth of human contact and companionship. To develop the language of touch is to improve upon the ease and confidence with which you handle your baby, and through every tactile expression provide your baby with tangible evidence of a caring presence.

For a good beginning, the sooner the better is the best time to start – skin to skin contact from birth, bathing together, lying together, lots of stroking and regularly oiling and cleansing your baby's skin using your hands. The following section looks at what is best to use when oiling or massaging your baby. Chapter Two will then show you how to introduce massage to your newborn before moving into the full body routine for babies of two months and upwards.

The Skin

In the developing embryo, the outermost of the three embryonic cellular layers, the ectoderm, becomes the central nervous system and then develops in the form of skin to cover the body of the foetus. As our body's largest visible source of sensory perception, the skin provides a principal means of communication. A unique protective cover that provides moment to moment intelligence on the hospitality of our body's immediate environment, this exposed sphere of our central nervous system perceives heat, cold and tactile impressions and illuminates emotional and physiological changes that take place within the body. As a barrier against invasion by micro-organisms, your baby's skin acts as the first line of defence against surface injury and contains a reservoir of defensive elements capable of combating infection and healing deep disruptions.

What is the skin?

Our skin is alive. It forms two new layers every three hours and sheds its cells at the rate of a million or so every hour. It incorporates:

- more than 2 million sweat pores that eliminate wastes;
- 2,000 glands per square inch which secrete oil, vital to our skin's resilience, elasticity and resistance to infection;
- fifteen feet of blood vessels per square inch, making it a thermostatic miracle;
- some 5 million sensory cells, that give feeling, depth and substance to the world around us;
- and it stores water, sugar, calcium and aids the production of Vitamin D.

As an extension of the nervous system, our skin reveals our deepest emotions when it tingles with excitement, blushes with embarrassment, turns livid with anger, white with fear and so on. Equally effective are the symptoms or signs that the skin exhibits as indications of well-being, illness or infection: from the hot brow, cold sweats, rashes and eruptions, the pallors and shivers that reveal illness, to the glowing complexion of good health.

What to use and what to avoid

The baby's skin is finer, with far more sensory receptors than that of an adult, and the openings of the sweat and sebaceous glands and hair follicles render a baby's skin porous and capable of absorption. Consequently only the purest products with the most subtle aromas are appropriate. Soft cotton clothing is the most agreeable texture against a fine skin, in preference to synthetic fabrics like nylon which prevents the skin from 'breathing' or wool, which can be abrasive. As a general guide to substances used on your baby's skin, organic is best. Products derived from living structures like plants and vegetables that are easily assimilated within the body, rather than those that are mineral based, should be used.

Most commercial baby oils are mineral oils, and as derivatives of crude petroleum they contain no organic food value. Because they are not readily absorbed into the body, oils like this tend to lie on top of the skin and block its pores; this prevents the skin from breathing, and inhibits the secretions of the glands that keep the skin waterproof and resilient. Consequently mineral oils tend to dry your baby's skin. In contrast, a pure vegetable, fruit or nut oil is readily absorbed and contains properties that are beneficial.

Talcum powder is also of a mineral base and does not absorb readily into the body. In the 1980s the government of Puerto Rico banned talc in the manufacture of rice because of a suspected link with stomach cancer. Research conducted at the same time also suggested that this product caused tumours when dusted on broken or abraded skin (see *Your Skin and How to Live in It*, Dr Jerome Z. Litt). Not widely available in the UK (although it is in the United States), a medicated cornstarch or maize-based powder is a good organic alternative to talcum powder or calendula powder, which also contains a talcum powder base.

The vernix

Stimulation of the baby through the skin begins with the strong uterine contractions that precipitate birth. The 'primal rubbing' of the birth process confers firm, muscular impressions that – like massage – stimulate the peripheral and autonomic nervous systems, and the principal organs for survival. The vernix caseosa (a white, greasy substance) equivalent to the finest of all massage oils, covers the baby's skin to protect it from the liquid environment of the womb. The vernix, together with other secretions, helps facilitate a smoother negotiation of the birth canal during labour and remaining in varying degrees after birth, it provides a protective layer for the newborn.

Many tribal cultures leave the vernix on for two or three days, or if it has been disturbed, wash the baby by hand with warm water and replace the skin's cover by oiling it. Soap is rarely used, as it dries the skin and removes its protective elements and secretions. Usually if the baby is 'overdue' little of the vernix remains and the baby's skin tends to be dry. In this event, bathing the baby by hand in warm water and applying an appropriate oil such as grapeseed almond or coconut (see pages 32–3) will supplement the skin's natural oils and provide an element of protection.

In the West the vernix is often routinely removed at birth. It seems paradoxical that this rich source of vitamin K should be removed and then vitamin K given by injection (now a controversial issue) or orally administered immediately following birth. It is interesting to note that in hospitals that do not routinely remove the vernix, the incidence of skin infections in babies has been considerably reduced. Some of the more sensitive midwives that I know have discovered the hidden properties of the vernix and say that they rub it into their hands to make their skin soft.

Base massage oils

There are a variety of organic oils known to contain beneficial constituents which are highly recommended for baby massage. Primarily, the oil you use for massage acts as an intermediary to facilitate a smooth movement and prevent friction between your hands and your baby's skin. Other benefits of organic oils are: they allow the skin to breathe, do not inhibit its resilient qualities and are easily absorbed, together with any organic food value. The surface of the baby's skin is smooth and moist and continually renewed through the constant regeneration of healthy cells; a regular massage with a pure organic oil also penetrates the pores and cleanses the skin of its dead cells, giving it a healthy glow.

The following base massage oils are recommended for massage with babies and children. They are inexpensive and widely available from most supermarkets and health shops.

Grapeseed

Known for their purity and their easy absorption into the digestive system, grapes are often used in cleansing diets. As a fruit oil, grapeseed is light and scent-free. It is very popular, and probably the most compatible with fine skin and baby massage.

Sweet Almond

Introduced into Europe by the Greeks and into England in the sixteenth century, almond water was used extensively in Elizabethan cooking. As a nut oil, almond is light with a very mild fragrance.

Coconut oil

The coconut palm is native to Polynesia and Malaysia. It grows wild, and is widely cultivated for a variety of uses throughout the tropics. Coconut is a light nut oil with a very mild fragrance. It comes in a solid form, which prevents spillage, but it is easily liquidised in warm hands.

One of the purest methods of extracting massage oil from its organic source is called 'cold pressed'. This is when the nut or the fruit is pressed at its lowest possible temperature and then filtered through paper. This leaves the oil with more colour, aroma and flavour of the nut or seed from which it was extracted. Cold-pressed oils are not always available but, if you have the choice, they are preferable.

Finally, these base oils are all edible, so although you would not administer them to your baby internally, if your baby puts an oily hand into his mouth while being massaged with any of these oils, there is no cause for alarm – they will not harm his delicate digestive system.

SKIN TEST

Whatever oil – or combination of oils – you use, always test for a skin reaction first. This is easily done by applying it to a small area of your baby's skin and leaving it for thirty minutes. An allergic reaction usually consists of red blotches which will disappear within an hour or two. Should your baby be allergic to one of the base massage oils, try one of the others. If your baby is sensitive to them all, consult your paediatrician for an alternative.

Essential oils

As well as the base massage oils, essential oils can also be used in baby massage. For thousands of years before the manufacture of soaps, natural oils were used to perfume and massage the body. As the therapeutic properties of specific plants and herbs became recognised, they were employed in a variety of ways to soothe, invigorate and heal all manner of complaints. Of those that remain in constant use many, like Aspirin – which is derived from the bark of the willow tree – are present in modern medications.

An essential oil is a volatile aromatic oil that is extracted from various parts of a plant including the leaves, flowers, seeds, root, bark, wood, balsam, resin and peel, with an aroma similar to the plant itself. It possesses the healing properties of the source from which it has been extracted. Used in massage these oils are absorbed through the skin and transported throughout the body. This process is easily demonstrated by rubbing a clove of garlic on the palm of your hand; after a while the odour will appear on your breath.

Essential oils are highly refined and potent and should always be diluted into a base massage oil like grapeseed or almond. They are not recommended for use with very young babies, but well-diluted some can be used with babies from about two months onwards. About three drops of essential oil to four tablespoons of grapeseed or almond oil is appropriate. Should you put a few drops in your baby's bath water, remember to first dilute them in a tablespoonful (15 ml) of milk. Essential oils should on no account be taken internally, nor should they be used as a substitute for professional diagnosis and treatment.

Not all essential oils are suitable for babies but of those that are, the most useful are the following:

English Lavender

A traditional English herb, popular since the twelfth century. Essential oil of lavender has antiseptic qualities which offer an element of protection. It is cooling, stimulative and also acts as an insect repellant. Commonly used as an inhalant, it clears the nostrils and airways. Useful with coughs and colds and last thing at night if your baby has the 'snuffles'. Also recommended for use after immunisation, or if your baby is a bit 'off colour' to help resist further infections.

Constituents Linalol and lynalyl acetate, a hydroxyconmarin, herniarin eucalyptol, limonene, cineole geraniol.

Chamomile Roman

Widely used by the ancient Egyptians, essential oil of chamomile roman is noted for its calming and soothing elements. An anti-inflammatory and sedative, it calms the digestive system and also possesses antiseptic qualities. Often recommended for teething and fractiousness, colic and last thing at night to improve sleeping.

Constituents Azulene, esters of engelic and tiglic acids, antehmal, anthemene.

Teatree

This is an oil with powerful antiseptic qualities. It is recommended for soothing and healing minor skin infections although it should only be used with the consent of your doctor after a proper diagnosis.

Constituents Terpenes, cineol, sesquiterpenes, sesquiterpenic alcohols.

Rose

An oil with a very pleasant aroma, rose is expensive, but highly recommended for very dry skin.

Constituents Eugenol, farnesol and other acids, geranoil (or citronellol), linalool, nerol, nonylic aldehyde, rhodinol, stearoptene.

Frankincense

This oil also has a very pleasant aroma. Deeply relaxing, it is recommended to deepen and improve the breathing rhythm.

Constituents Ketonic alcohol, resinous matters, terpenes.

Myrrh

Myrrh is also recommended to improve breathing. It is used to soothe inflammation of the bronchial tubes and help eliminate mucus.

Constituents Acids, alcohols, aldehydes, sugars, phenols, resins, terpenes.

CHAPTER TWO

Handling with Confidence

In many cultures,
the newborn enters the world
gently, in a warmed darkened room;
breathing is stimulated not with a slap,
but by a rhythmic massage
or a gentle pat.

JUDITH GOLDSMITH
Childbirth Wisdom

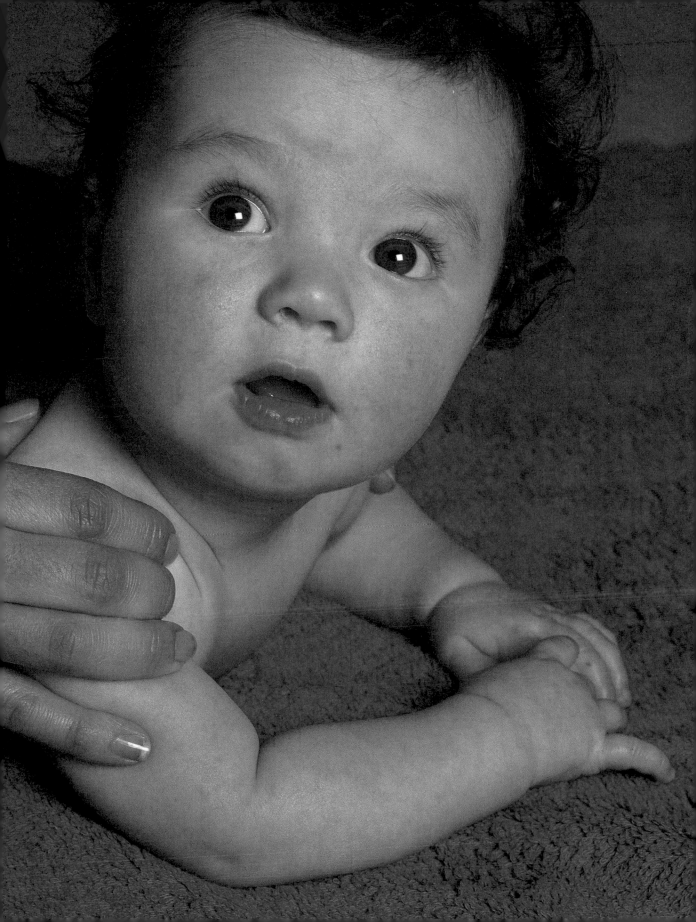

Preparing to Massage

Birth to Two Months

As we have seen in the previous chapter, the transition for a baby from the security of the womb to the outside world may not be an easy one. A newborn is highly sensitive to her new environment, and it is most important that in the time immediately following the birth that this transition is made as comfortable and as smooth as possible for her.

I have been fortunate in being able to be present at a number of births, including the birth of my own two children, my godchildren, those of some of my closest friends and some others in need of support. In all of these the mother-to-be made it very clear that due care and consideration was to be given to the needs and sensitivities of her newborn baby.

Given a normal labour and delivery this usually meant:

- not cutting the cord until it had stopped pulsating;
- continued body contact – skin to skin with the mother;
- due sensitivity if clearing the baby's nostrils and airways;
- subdued sound, lighting and aromas.

Immediately following the birth there was a variable period of time given for the mother, father and newborn baby to be with each other, a time to assimilate the unspecified characteristics of their new relationship.

Anointing the newborn with oils

The ceremonial bathing of the newborn baby seems an appropriate time to give a very soft massage. (Bathtime has long been the most popular occasion for massage and because of this association with bathing, massage has also been known as shampooing!) First, wash your baby in warm water to leave as much of the vernix intact as possible and then gently rub your baby with one of the recommended oils. This helps to maintain an extra element of protection and offers your baby some reassurance through touch. Use the oil in the same way as if you were using soap and then pat your baby dry with a warm, soft towel. If this proves to be impractical following the baby's birth, the same can be done later and repeated as frequently as you wish.

If your baby's skin is very dry at birth and it is not possible to oil him, a tablespoon of olive or grapeseed oil can be added to his bath. Keep the oil away from your baby's eyes as it may blur his vision. (It has been suggested that soapy water splashing into your baby's eyes can give him a fear of being bathed and later a subconscious fear of water.)

Most babies also enjoy having their head, upper back, the base of their spine and lower back stroked. Done with or without oil, dressed or undressed, and as frequently as you feel inclined, this is a nice way to begin baby massage.

Benefits of baby massage

Massaging your baby will provide a whole range of benefits, including the following, both for you and for her.

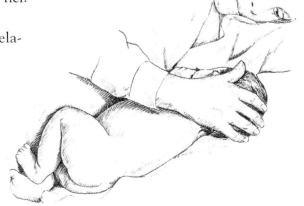

- Opens a totally new dimension in your relationship with your child.
- Provides unique, meditative interval for direct physical contact and affectionate expression.
- Fosters more trust and confidence in you and your baby.
- Develops your confidence in your ability to handle your baby.

- Induces a more relaxed state in your baby.
- Encourages muscular coordination.
- Creates ease throughout the body.
- Calms the emotions and relieves trauma.
- Soothes the body and relieves pain.
- Provides an antidote for hypertension and anxiety.
- Helps promote sleep.
- Stimulates your baby's immune system. } Both immature
- Stimulates your baby's circulation. } at birth.
- Aids digestion and elimination.
- Visibly improves the texture of the skin.
- Deep-cleanses the pores of the skin.
- Helps retain the skin's elasticity and resilient qualities.
- Is the perfect preparation for coordinate movement and mobility.
- Is a natural response to your baby's inherent need for tactile stimulation.
- Fosters fluid, relaxed movement.
- Provides a unique period of mutual pleasure, once your baby begins to anticipate her massage.

Contra-indications

Do not wake your baby for a massage, and never massage him against his will. Make sure that your touch is always relaxed, smooth and gentle and **never** force any of the movements. Always stop if your baby gets upset, give him what he wants and return to the massage when he is ready and willing. When your baby is sitting and starting to crawl you can massage him sitting, but he will resist strongly – and rightly so – if you try to hold him down.

Illness

Your baby will probably not want to be massaged if he is feeling poorly, although he may want to be held and carried. Seek professional help if your baby is unwell.

Left Stroking your baby's head and back is a good way to begin baby massage.

Immunisation

It is usually best to wait for forty-eight hours to see how immunisation will affect your child. If she appears to be fine, massage avoiding the injection site. After about a week, if it is no longer sensitive, you can begin gently to massage the affected area to disperse any 'lump'.

Skin disorders and infections

It is important not to spread or exacerbate the condition so seek professional advice first.

N.B. IF ANY DOUBT SEEK PROFESSIONAL ADVICE.

Getting ready to massage

Our hands are centres of feeling and expression. If you want your baby in the palms of your hands then you must use them and feel with them.

Massaging your baby provides you with a meditative period, a unique time to focus on your baby through your hands. If you allow yourself to become distracted, your baby could get distracted. Shake your hands from your wrists before you start as this is a good way to relax and loosen them up. If you observe yourself becoming distracted during the massage, come back to this, shake your hands out again and turn your attention away from your thoughts and back to feeling. Whilst massaging, look into your baby's eyes and talk or sing to her. You can describe the actions or the part of her body being massaged to her.

It is most important to have enough oil on your hands at all times during your baby's massage. Keep replenishing your oil, and rather use too much than too little. At the end of the massage, you can always wipe away any surplus; this serves the dual purpose of facilitating massage and cleaning the skin. As a pure vegetable oil gets absorbed into the skin, you must keep replacing it. The baby's skin should glisten and your hands must glide easily while maintaining a firm, but relaxed hold. If you do not use enough oil, the sensation of being massaged could well be unpleasant for your baby.

M A K E   S U R E :

- your hands are clean and warm;
- your nails or jewellery cannot scratch your baby's skin;
- the room is warm and draught-free;
- your baby is not hungry and not full;
- you will remain undisturbed for about an hour;
- you are sitting comfortably and relaxed;
- your baby is lying on a soft, clean, cotton surface, the combination of wool and oil may irritate the skin;
- you keep the oil away from your baby's face as it can blur vision if it gets into the eyes.

Always stop if your baby cries. You cannot force a baby to relax. This is a time for mutual pleasure, not a battle of wills, so it is better to give your baby what she wants and return to massage when she becomes more receptive.

Your position

Before you begin to massage your baby, make sure that you are sitting comfortably with your neck and shoulders relaxed. Try either of the following:

Sit on the edge of a cushion with your legs and feet in front of you.

Sit on your feet, on a cushion.

Keep your position comfortable, change it if you need to, or break for a minute or two and stretch your legs if you are stiff. Also, to keep your hands relaxed, remember to shake them from time to time and to give them a 'rub' together.

Breathing and relaxation

Last, but by no means least, check your breathing rhythm to assess your general state of relaxation. If you are holding your belly in and breathing only with your chest, you are withholding your breath, a condition associated with stress and anxiety. To alleviate this, gently draw in your tummy to push the air out with your exhalation and on your inhalation relax your tummy and let it expand with your chest. This is your natural breathing rhythm, one in which the chest and belly work in harmony to give you the maximum supply of oxygen for a minimum of physical effort.

Continue to practise this whenever you remember it, wherever you are, and it will become spontaneous, considerably reducing your feelings of anxiety and the ill effects of stress which all too easily can affect your relationship with your child.

If your baby does not respond well ...

Don't be discouraged. Either keep practising the following preliminary routine, or introduce the full body routine for a few minutes at a time, starting with the feet; then when this is accepted, the legs and belly and so on, slowly, little by little, day by day, adding to your routine. Persevere, work with your baby. It will be well worth it. Quite often those babies who do not respond well at the beginning are the ones who eventually enjoy being massaged the most.

If there is a particular area of the body where your baby consistently resists being massaged, leave it and 'loosen it up' first. For instance, if it is the tummy, whenever nappy changing tickle it and give it a little rub; or if it's the arms, from time to time clap your baby's hands together to a nursery rhyme and give them a little shake, before including them in your usual routine.

INTRODUCING A LIGHT MASSAGE

Once your baby is happy to be undressed and enjoys being naked you can introduce a light massage lying together with your baby on a soft towel.

1. With relaxed, well-oiled hands, stroke down the side of your baby's body from the shoulder over the arm, chest, hip and leg. Repeat for about a minute.

2. Then, with your baby lying in the same position, using a clockwise movement, stroke around the back of your baby's chest. Repeat slowly for about a minute.

3. Massage the back of your baby's hips and base of the spine, again clockwise, for about a minute. Now repeat these steps for the other side of the body.

4. If your baby is happy to lie on her back, stroke gently down the front of the body from the shoulders to the feet for a minute or two.

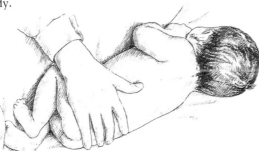
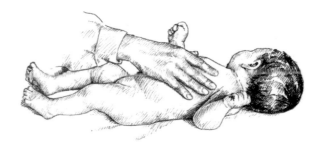

5. If your baby is happy to lie on her tummy, or belly to belly on yours, stroke gently hand over hand down the back, from the shoulders to the base of the spine for about a minute or two.

Once your baby has become used to this ten-minute routine, then move on and introduce the full baby massage routine (pages 48-73).

The Baby Massage Routine

Two Months and Onwards

Having completed the preliminaries, and when you and your baby are both ready, you can start the full massage routine. Begin with your baby lying on his back facing you.

Your baby's legs

The legs are our body's roots and they have to be strong enough to support the body and flexible enough to allow movement. You will probably notice your baby exercising his legs by repetitive kicking. Bending and straightening them in this way makes the joints flexible and strengthens the muscles of the legs and lower back in preparation for upright postures and mobility. Sitting and standing involves balance. And balance is only possible through a strong foundation or when the body's weight is evenly distributed downwards through the body's roots. Good sitting, standing and moving posture comes from strong legs and flexible hip, knee and ankle joints.

Making sure your hands are
well oiled, take your baby's leg
and shake it gently. Now
firmly and evenly pull the leg
hand over hand through your
palms and fingers from the
thigh to the foot. Repeat this
several times on the same leg.
'Pulling someone's leg' is
associated with good nature
and a sense of humour so this is
often a good place to start or to come
back to, especially if you keep it playful and from
time to time give the legs a gentle shake.

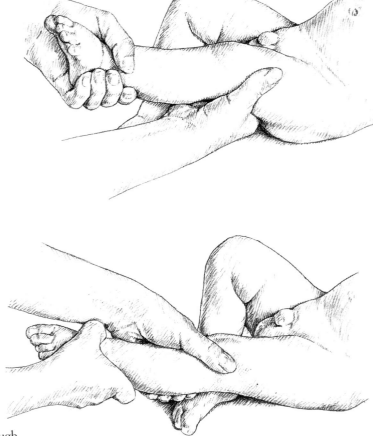

Now hold the ankle with your
inside hand and with your outside
hand massage down and around
from the front to the back of the
thigh and up again, keeping your
hand on the leg above the knee.
Repeat this several times.

Making sure your hands are
relaxed from the wrists, pull
the calf and foot hand over
hand through your palms. As
one hand reaches the foot, the
other starts simultaneously at
the back of the knee. Repeat
this several times. Again pull
the whole leg hand over hand through
your palms. Repeat this a few times and shake
the leg gently.

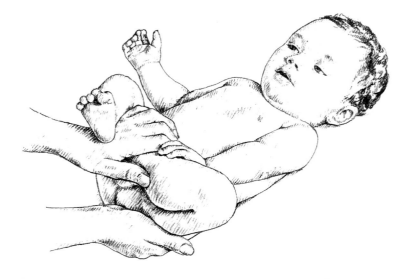

Now bend the knee outwards and push the leg gently sideways to the floor. Hold the leg in this position with your outside hand and with the palm of your other hand, gently squeeze and massage the inside of the thigh. Repeat this several times. Again, give the leg a gentle shake and pull it hand over hand through your palms two or three times.

Letting the knee bend outwards, gently push the foot and inside of the ankle on to your baby's tummy. Holding this with your inside hand, use the palm of your other hand to massage around the buttock and back thigh. Do this several times.

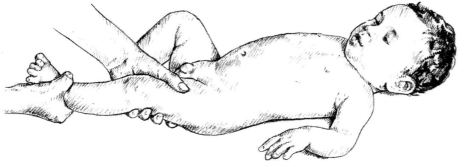

Again straighten the leg, giving it a gentle shake and pull it hand over hand through your palms two or three times. Now stop. Shake out your hands and relax your shoulders. Make sure you are sitting comfortably before repeating all of these movements for the other leg.

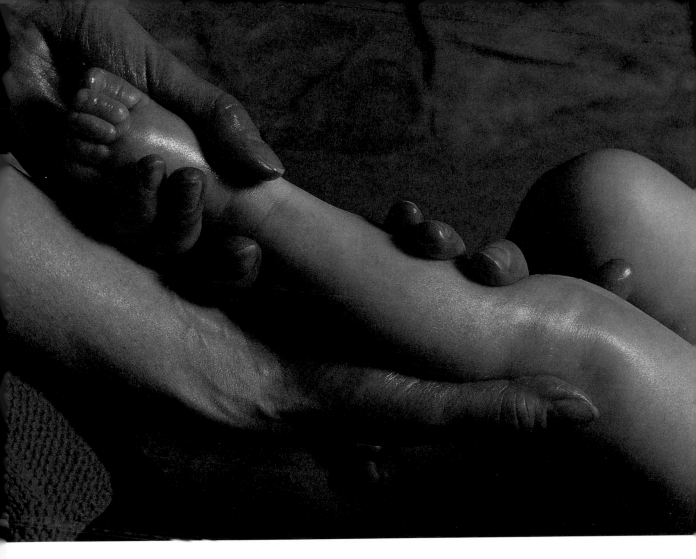

Above Good posture comes from strong legs and flexible joints.

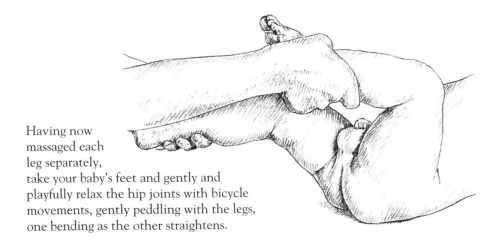

Having now
massaged each
leg separately,
take your baby's feet and gently and
playfully relax the hip joints with bicycle
movements, gently peddling with the legs,
one bending as the other straightens.

Replenish your oil and, placing your hands on the inside thighs, pull down and around the thigh to pull down the back of the knee, calf and foot. Repeat this several times, pulling down over the back of your baby's knees as he straightens his legs.

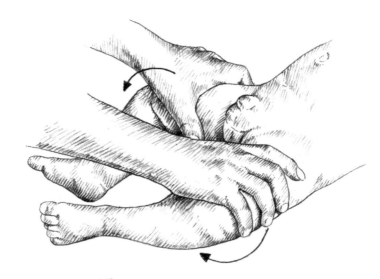

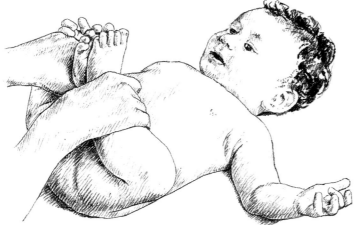

Repeat the bicycle movement three or four times, clap the soles of your baby's feet together, kiss them and blow on them.

Then letting the knees bend outwards with the soles of the feet together, gently push both feet on to his tummy and hold them there with one hand.

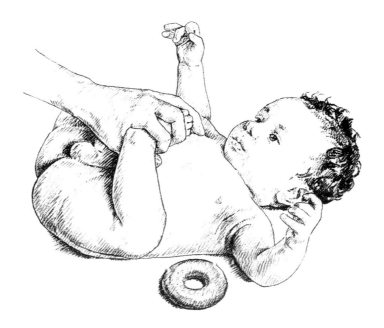

Relax your baby in this
position by gently rocking
him from side to side by his
feet. Sustaining this rocking
movement, now massage all
around the base of the spine
with the palm of your free
hand.

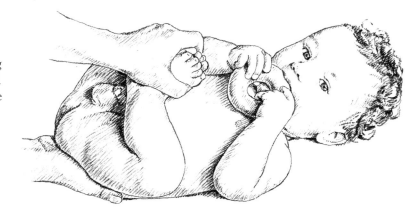

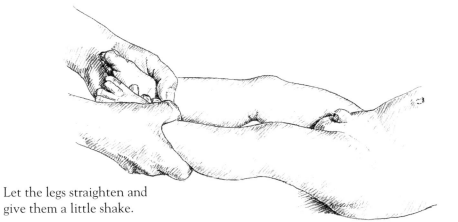

Let the legs straighten and
give them a little shake.

To finish the leg massage,
replenish your oil and, using
the palms of your hands,
pull down both sides of the
body from under the arms
over the sides of the chest,
hips and legs. Repeat four or
five times.

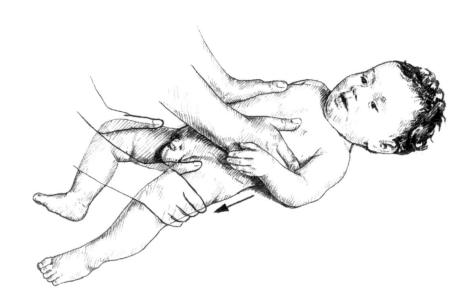

Your baby's belly

Nourished through the umbilicus, the belly is the very centre of existence for the babe in the womb. At birth this umbilical connection continues to pulsate and keeps the baby secure until the child's own life-sustaining organs function for themselves: a perfect physiological exchange, as the old environment continues to lend support until the baby is physiologically secure in the new.

As a centre of intuition, our own gut feelings often predict an outcome of events with more accuracy than our intellect. Recent medical developments reveal the nerve cells in the small intestine to be nearly as prolific as

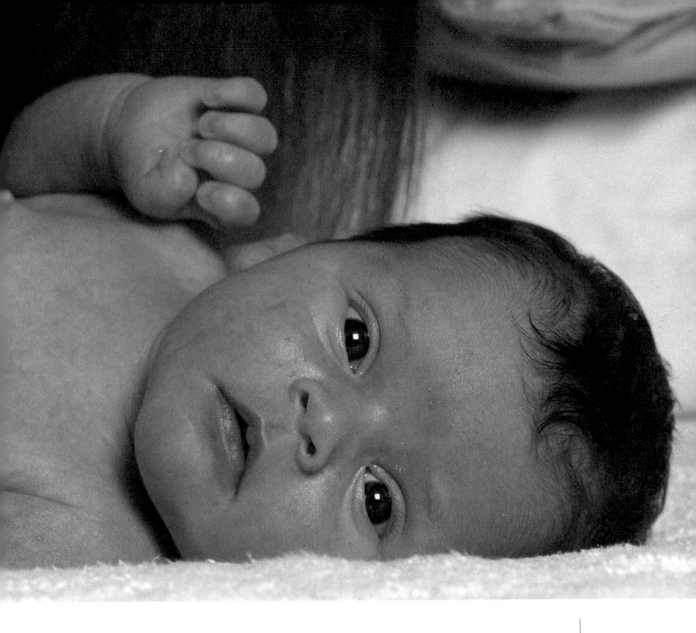

Above *Massaging the belly is very comforting for your baby.*

those of the brain itself. Because of this, this area is now known as 'the little brain'.

In the East the belly has long been revered: by the Japanese as the *Onaka*, the honoured middle; and by the Japanese and Chinese as the centre of *Chi*, a source of great energy utilised for self-healing and self-defence. As an emotional centre, the belly tightens in response to fear, stress and anxiety and relaxes with tranquility.

Starting with your fingertips, massage clockwise in circles around the naval. Do this lightly several times.

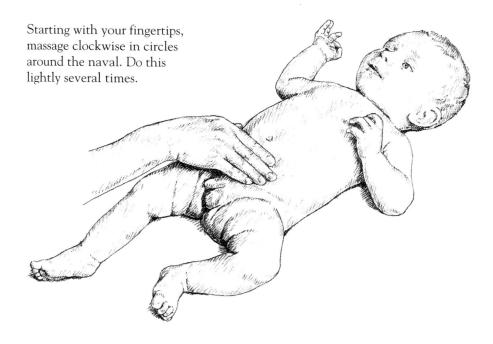

Now, using just the relaxed weight of your hand, with the palm of your hand covering your baby's belly, again massage clockwise, keeping your hand open, your fingers extending over the lower chest, the heel of your hand above the pubic bone. Repeat several times, but do not push downwards, just use the relaxed weight of your hand.

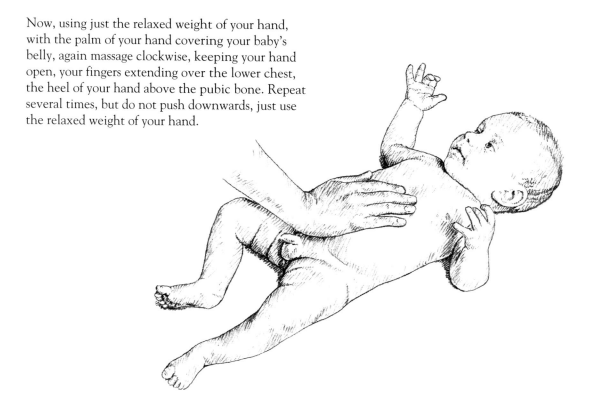

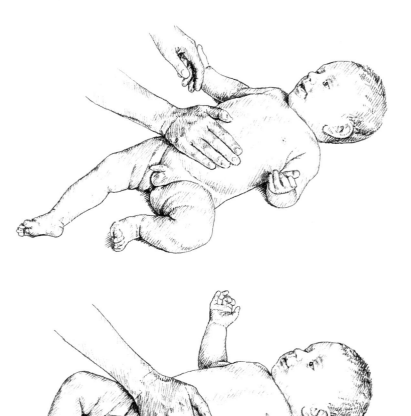

Next cup your hand and lay your hand horizontally across your baby's belly and push in sideways, gently, from between the hip and the lowest rib. You do this with the heel of your hand (left). Pull back gently with the pads of your fingers (below); this stimulates the ascending and descending colon. You can also rock your baby from side to side using this same technique, but ensure that you push in sideways and not downwards. If you push downwards, and there is any obstruction, it will increase the discomfort. If you push in sideways and there is any discomfort your baby can roll away.

Using this same technique, massage into the side of the belly, hand over hand on the left and the right side. Unless your baby has been fed recently, his belly should be soft and malleable and feel like marshmallow.

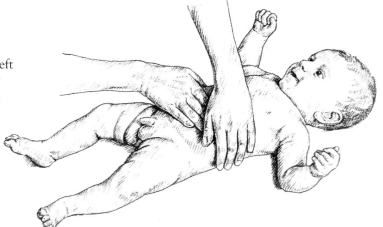

Your baby's chest and shoulders

Residing in the chest, the beat of the heart and the rhythm of breathing converge into the pulse of life. Long considered the centre of love and courage, this area is also associated with grief and longing, and the great wave of breath that precedes our feelings of elation or self-satisfaction is the same wave that breaks into tears of sorrow.

Either way, to breathe is to feel, and the very word 'inspire' means both to 'breathe in' and 'to arouse feeling'. Alternatively, to breathe little is to feel little, and one of the ways in which our bodies cope with trauma is to stop breathing, or inhibit the breath to diminish the sensation of pain. As an emotional residence of grief and longing, the sensations mostly associated with pain in the heart are more accurately associated with the muscular constriction of the chest and throat that accompanies bouts of repressed or prolonged crying. Mobilise your baby's breath and you will generate life and feeling. An open chest and shoulders, combined with a relaxed belly, inspire the maximum volume of oxygen, the very spirit of life.

Make sure your hands are relaxed and well oiled. Place your hands on the centre of the chest and massage upwards and outwards over the shoulders and back to the centre of the chest again. Feel the shoulders in the palms of your hands. Repeat this several times.

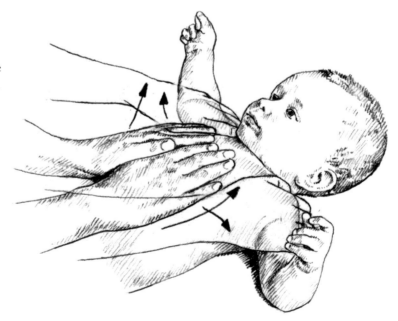

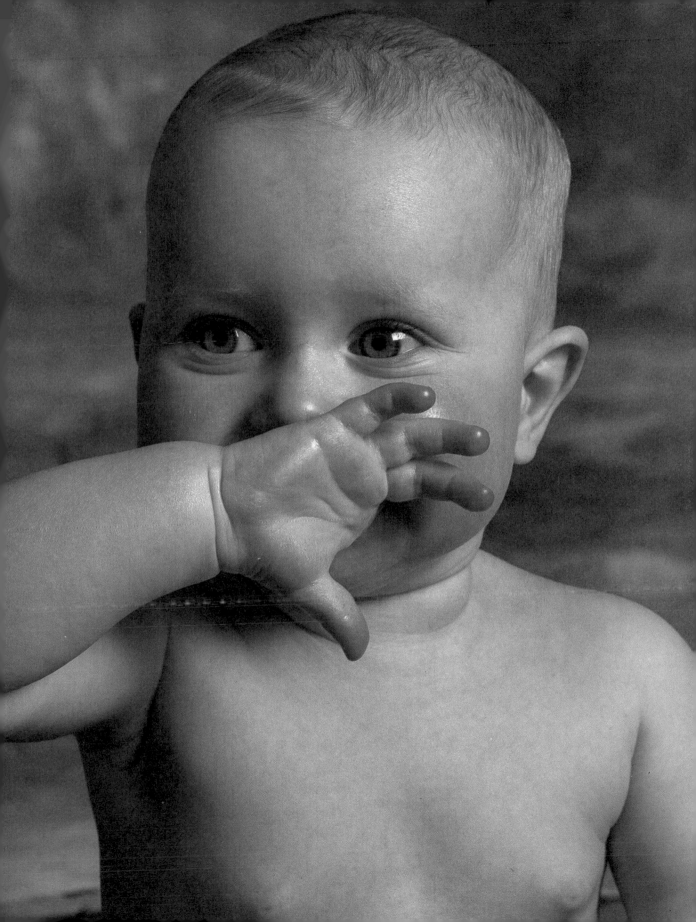

Next, place your hands on the centre of the chest and massage upwards and outwards, over the shoulders, and draw the arms down vertically through the centre of your palms. Repeat this several times.

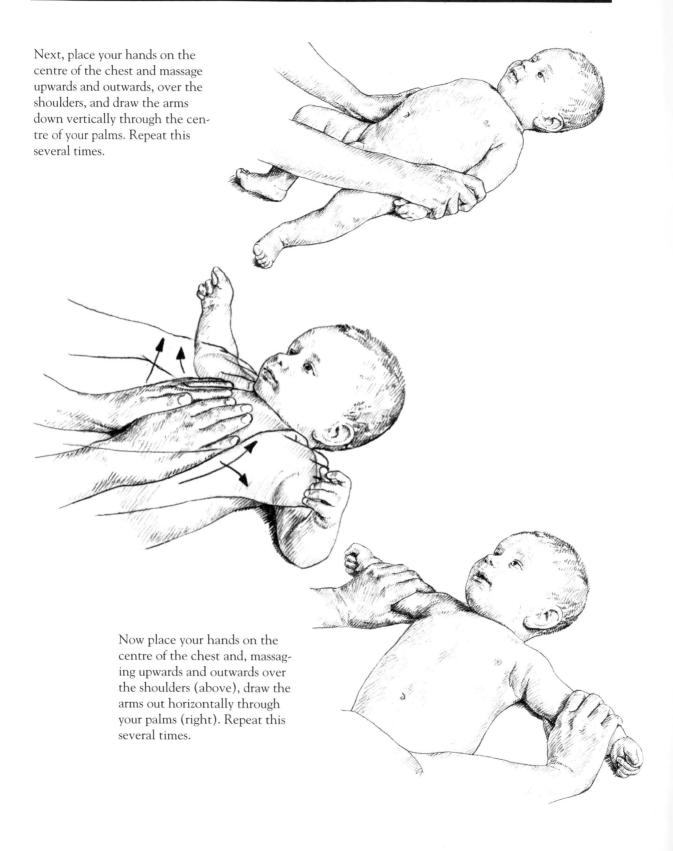

Now place your hands on the centre of the chest and, massaging upwards and outwards over the shoulders (above), draw the arms out horizontally through your palms (right). Repeat this several times.

With your hands on the inside of
the elbow joints, and your thumbs
on the elbows, tap the arms gently but quickly against the floor,
to relax the arms and shoulders.

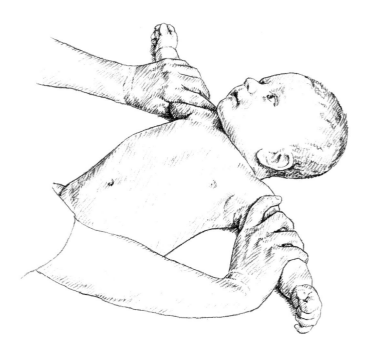

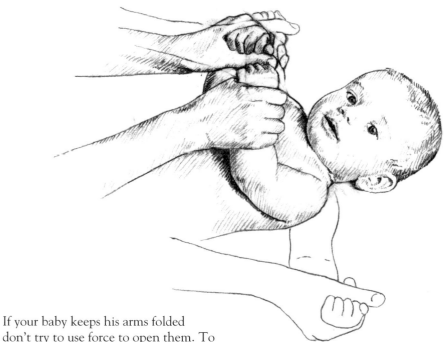

If your baby keeps his arms folded
don't try to use force to open them. To
encourage them to open clap the hands
together playfully, but quickly, and little
by little then open them.

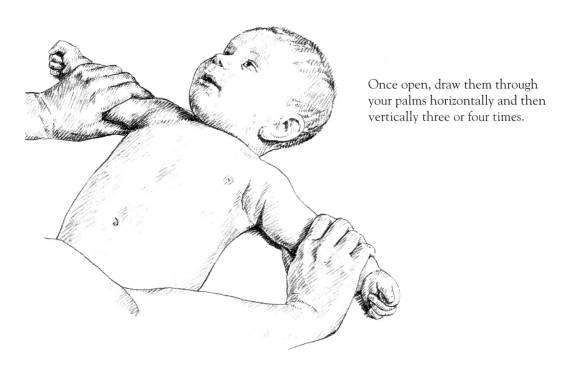

Once open, draw them through your palms horizontally and then vertically three or four times.

Finally, stroke down the body from the front of the shoulders over the chest, hips and legs. Do this three or four times.

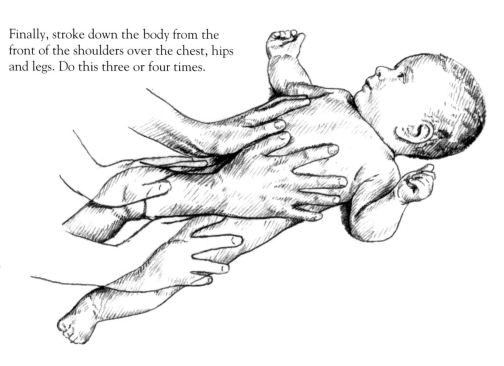

Right *Massage helps to open your child's chest and shoulders.*

Your baby's feet

The feet are a living masterpiece of architectural engineering – the toes spread for stability, the weight centred on to a sprung arch, the squat heel setting down firmly with every step forward. Generally we walk or run, and only discover how easily we perform such a hazardous activity when we stumble or, say, miss the last step on a flight of stairs and with a shock realise our weight is no longer cushioned.

Massage of the feet, known as reflexology, is one of the oldest forms of massage. The ancient reflexologists realised that massaging the feet could effect a feeling of relaxation that pervades the whole body. For babies (and for your partner) this can be quite a nice introduction to massage and a non-intrusive way to soothe or stimulate recovery from illness.

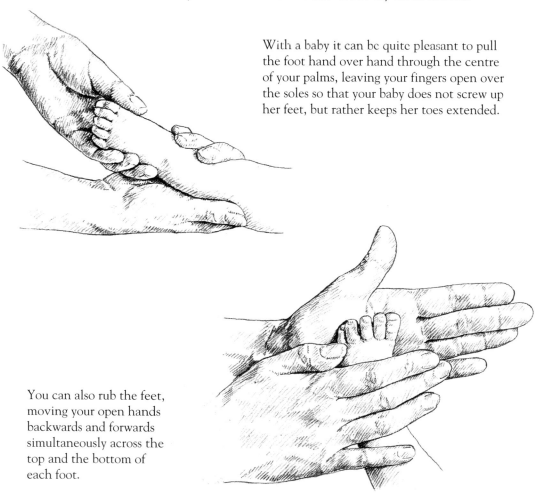

With a baby it can be quite pleasant to pull the foot hand over hand through the centre of your palms, leaving your fingers open over the soles so that your baby does not screw up her feet, but rather keeps her toes extended.

You can also rub the feet, moving your open hands backwards and forwards simultaneously across the top and the bottom of each foot.

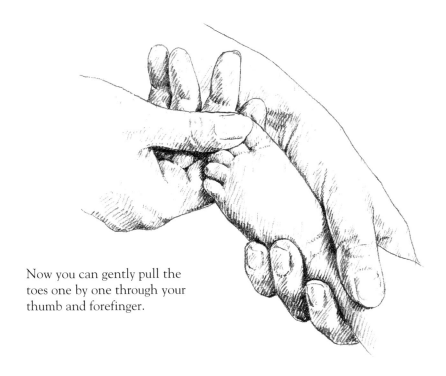

Now you can gently pull the toes one by one through your thumb and forefinger.

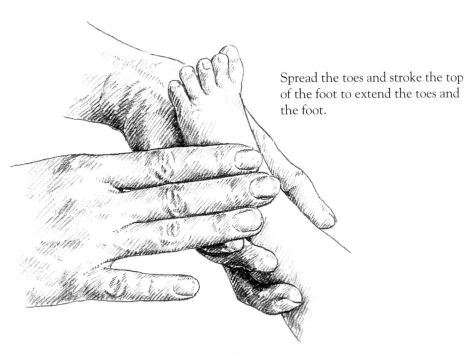

Spread the toes and stroke the top of the foot to extend the toes and the foot.

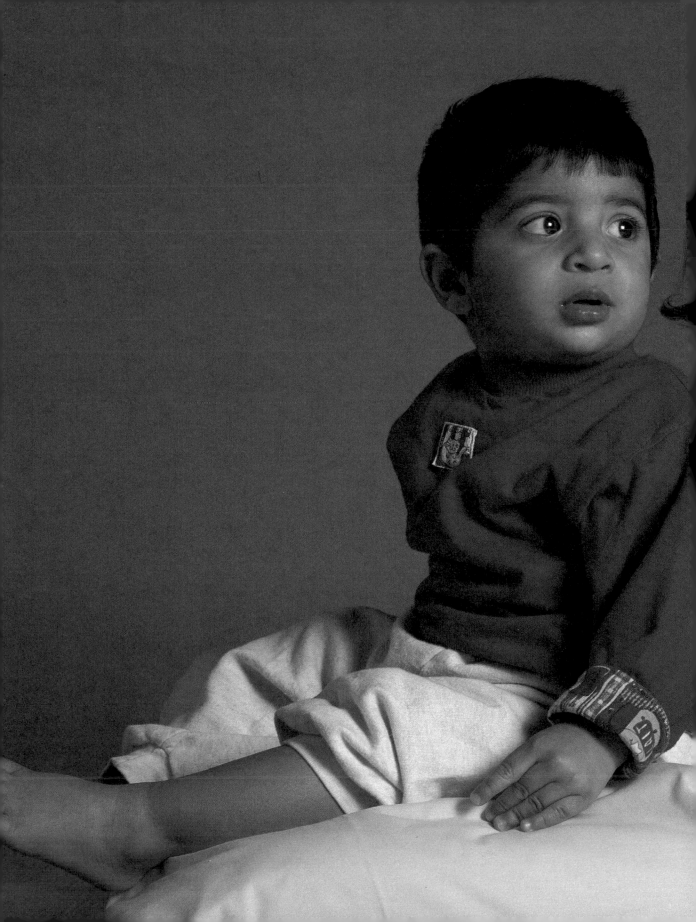

Your baby's back and backbone

The spine is the central pillar of support for the head, heart, lungs and digestive organs. It is a hollow, flexible column of thirty-three bones, making four equally opposing curves to balance and counterbalance the weight it supports. A veritable 'tree of life', the spine houses the nervous system and from each of its joints two root nerves project and multiply to serve every living part of the body. The strength and flexibility of the spine is crucial to:

- the health of the nervous system;
- the body's posture and its relationship with gravity;
- the flexibility of the chest and breathing capacity;
- the relaxation of the abdomen and digestive ease.

The body is as strong as the back that supports it, and from the very first days of life your baby will begin to strengthen the muscles that support his spine, and make his spine more flexible.

To begin the back massage, lie your baby on his tummy with his feet towards you.

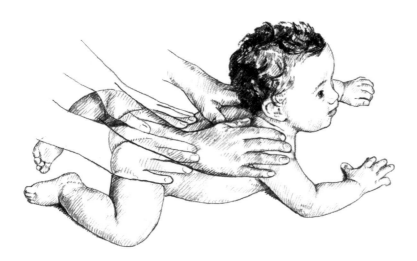

Using lots of oil and the palms of your hands, stroke down your baby's back from the back of the shoulders to the base of the spine. Repeat several times.

Previous page Back massage helps to strengthen the muscles that support the spine and encourages good sitting posture.

Now cup your hands and, using just the weight of your relaxed hands, pat the back quickly and firmly from the back of the chest and shoulders down to the base of the spine. (All babies love having their backs patted; this is just an extension of this movement which will tighten and strengthen these muscles.) Repeat percussion two or three times.

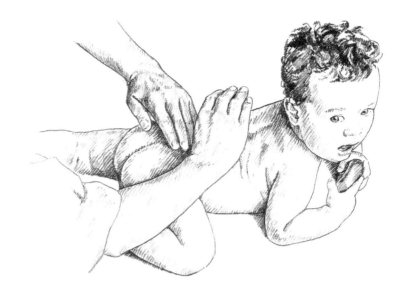

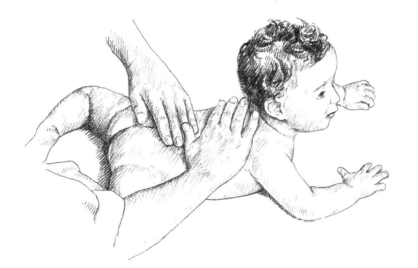

Again, stroke hand over hand down the back from the back of the shoulders to the base of the spine. Repeat this three or four times.

Replenish your oil and gently pull one arm downwards and backwards in line with your baby's body. Hold the arm with one hand and place your other hand across the shoulder.

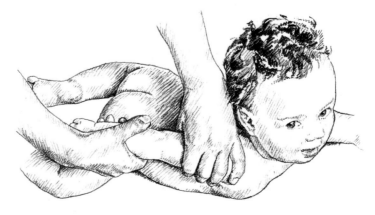

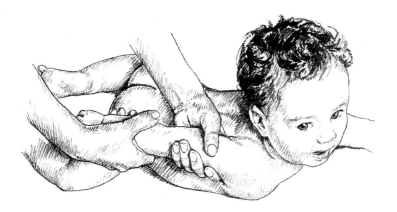

Draw your hand over the shoulder and down the arm, using your palm and fingers. Keeping the arm in this position, draw it hand over hand, through your palms, three or four times. Replace the hand and arm back in front of the baby's body. Now do the same with the other arm.

Now replenish your oil and do both arms simultaneously by placing your hands on the front of the chest, drawing them over the shoulders (right) and drawing the arms back through your palms (below left) and then letting them go. Repeat this movement three or four times, then place the arms and hands back in front of the body (below right). This movement is something that babies do for themselves at some point in their development; it greatly strengthens the upper back, and opens the top of the chest and shoulders – vital to good posture.

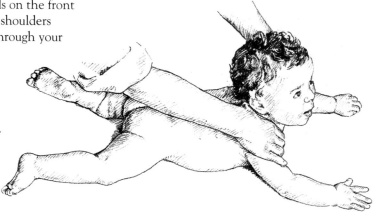

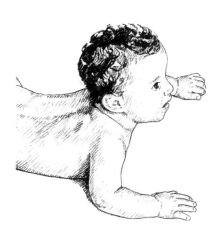

Take care when you do both arms simultaneously not to lift your baby up. Just pull the arms through your palms – let them go – and repeat.

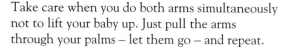

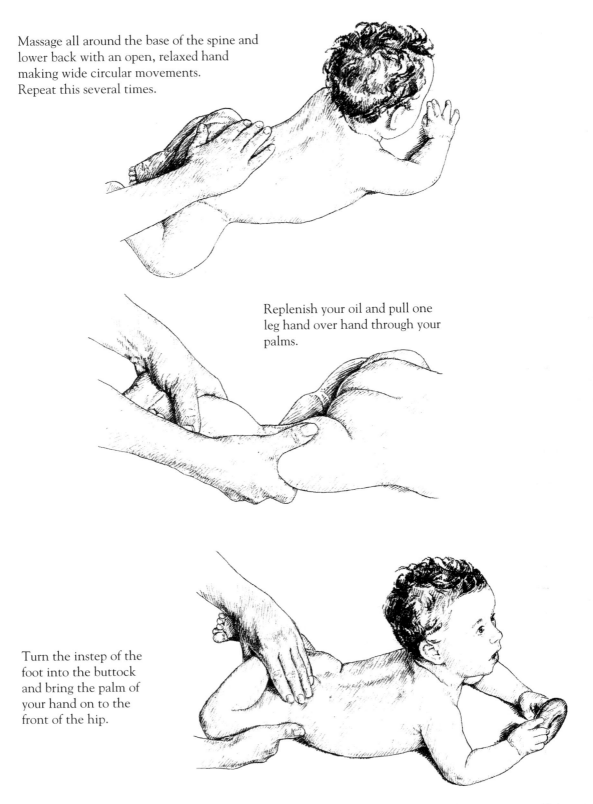

Massage all around the base of the spine and lower back with an open, relaxed hand making wide circular movements. Repeat this several times.

Replenish your oil and pull one leg hand over hand through your palms.

Turn the instep of the foot into the buttock and bring the palm of your hand on to the front of the hip.

Now draw your hand
backwards and forwards
over the thigh. Repeat
this three or four times.

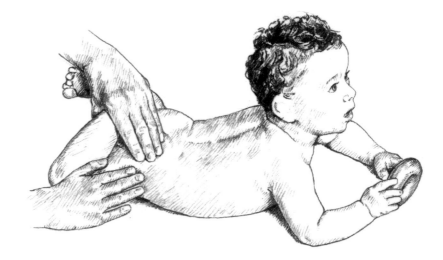

Next, let the leg straighten and
pull it hand over hand again
through your palms two or three
times. Repeat for the other leg.

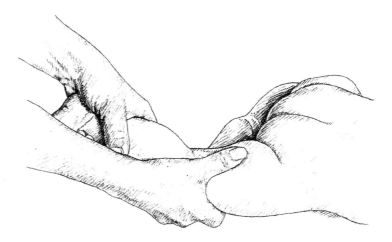

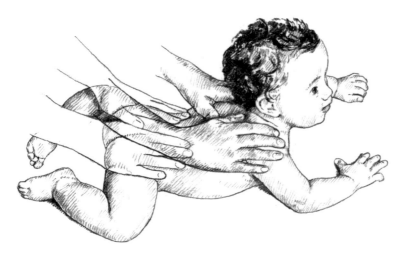

To complete your baby's
massage, put both your
hands on the back of the
shoulders and, using just the
weight of your relaxed
hands, draw them down the
back and the back of the
legs. Repeat this two or
three times.

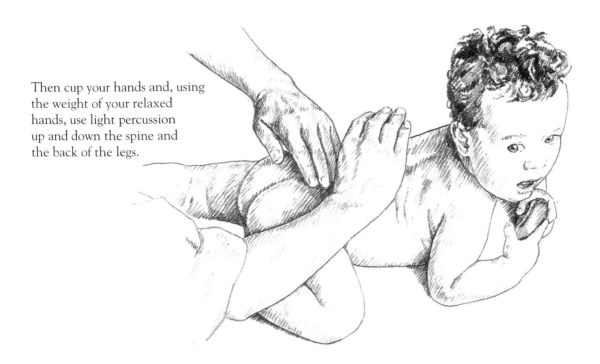

Then cup your hands and, using the weight of your relaxed hands, use light percussion up and down the spine and the back of the legs.

When you have finished the routine, wipe your baby with a soft, clean towel to cleanse the skin and remove any excess oil. Wash your hands to remove any excess oil before you replace your baby's nappy.

The whole routine should take no longer than twenty minutes. It can be repeated as often as you like. Last thing at night can encourage a deeper sleeping rhythm.

REMINDERS

- Keep your hands relaxed.
- Turn off your thoughts.
- Check your breathing is relaxed.
- Replenish your oil frequently.
- Do not continue if your baby cries.
- Look into your baby's eyes.
- Sing, talk to your baby.
- You can stop at any time, return and continue where you left off.
- You do not have to complete the whole routine.

CHAPTER THREE

Massage, Posture and Mobility

God guard me from the
thoughts men think in the mind alone,
he that sings a lasting song
thinks in a marrow bone.

WILLIAM BUTLER YEATS
The King of the Great Clock Tower

Growth and Development

Your baby's development depends upon the maturation of her nervous system and the neurological connections that precede all phases of growth. Consequently, no amount of persuasion can initiate progress without the development of the nervous system.

A child develops through her continuous interaction with her environment. Initially, usually the mother and sometimes the father provides the main basis for interaction and then a secure base from which the baby can venture further.

The young infant knows nothing of the world and consequently moving into the unknown is possible only when there is a secure matrix to which the child can make an immediate return, the younger the child, the more immediate and constant this return.

Joseph Chiltern Pearce
Magical Child

Learning through exploration

Learning takes place through exploratory activities that yield an interesting experience. The child then repeats the activity that leads to the experience, and through constant rehearsal and practise maps the scenario. This then provides the basis for further exploration and development. It is from simple isolated acts like grasping and glancing that intelligence develops. Grasping becomes holding, hand to mouth becomes seeing, holding and transferring as in hand with object to mouth and so on – each new acquisition being dependent on the last.

Manipulative play encourages the practice and skilful use of the hands and the coordination of the hands and eyes and the development of mental faculties. Initially, the baby's perceptual abilities are more developed than her movements. As voluntary movement begins and perceptual abilities coordinate, the baby's responses and acquired skills indicate increasing degrees of general understanding.

Concurrent with her development, the baby stretches her body and limbs and creates a wonderful degree of flexible movements. Simultaneously she strengthens her back in readiness for upright posture and movement and then sitting, crawling, standing and walking, the baby begins weightlifting; by lifting and carrying her ever-increasing bodyweight she strengthens rapidly.

The general development of the child is marked by common steps of progression, but the age at which she makes these accomplishments has no bearing upon her potential intelligence or physical abilities. All children vary in their rate of development. Some crawl early and walk late, while others crawl late and walk early and so on. (Einstein didn't speak until he was four.)

Between the obvious achievements that mark progression there are far more subtle developments that benefit the child as a whole being. Experience is a prime factor in learning, and what the baby needs is to be given the opportunities in order to practise and progress in her own time.

Similarly, the establishing of routines and modes of social behaviour should also take account of the needs and abilities of the child.

Do not mistake the compliance
of a child for growth. It may be convenient
to push the baby into accepting civilised
standards, but it is far better to encourage the
baby's innate tendencies at an age when
she can understand.

D.W. WINNICOTT
The Child, the Family and the Outside World

Understanding your baby

The value of a secure, affectionate relationship with a parent or caretaker during childhood is incalculable. Although it can be said to reap its own rewards, the labour of early childcare can be arduous, and in ceasing to be a labour of love, at best it can become mechanical, at worst, abusive. Lack of adequate support for the family, parental stress and depression, poor social conditions, poverty and malnutrition, can all have a detrimental affect upon the growth and development of the child. Understanding your baby's development, both physically and emotionally, can help you to maintain a happy, relaxed relationship with your child and avoid some of the frustrations which could hamper your relationship. The following section will help you to recognise some common basic achievements and how they take place.

Early Days

From a few weeks of age onwards your baby may
show quite an interest in your face and may scan
it. His smile in response to your voice will
increase daily and from about two months
on he will show a greater interest in his
immediate environment.

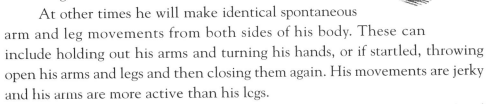

Lying on his back the newborn baby
keeps his limbs folded, his head turned to
one side, with his hips and knees open (see
right). When awake, he moves his hands, arms
and legs, involuntarily opening his hands and
stretching his limbs.

At other times he will make identical spontaneous
arm and leg movements from both sides of his body. These can
include holding out his arms and turning his hands, or if startled, throwing
open his arms and legs and then closing them again. His movements are jerky
and his arms are more active than his legs.

Lying on his front the newborn baby lies on his tummy, with his head
turned to one side, pelvis raised, knees open and drawn up under his body
(see below).

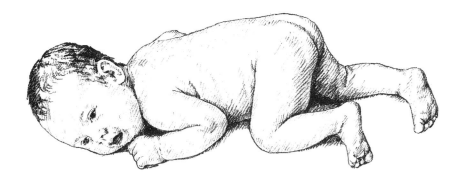

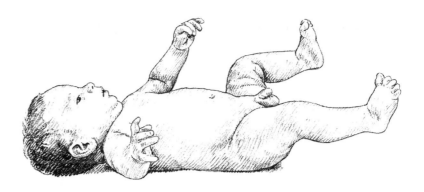

At around the age of one month in the same position he may momentarily lift his chin from the floor. His legs will be straighter and he will kick them. At two months his legs will have straightened more. Also both his arms and his legs will be more active and less jerky.

At about three months he will lie on his back with his head held in midline (see above). He will wave his arms and bring his hands together in midline over his chest and chin. He can kick his legs vigorously, mostly alternately but sometimes both legs together. His movements are now smoother and more continuous. At this time he may also lift his head and shoulders from the floor, bearing his weight on his forearms, with his body straight.

Between two and three months the baby will begin to 'play' and usually the first toy is a rattle. Mobiles are also popular, especially faces, which can be made easily.

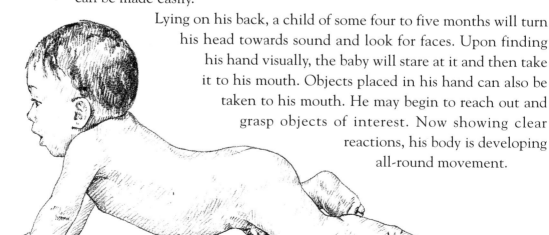

Lying on his back, a child of some four to five months will turn his head towards sound and look for faces. Upon finding his hand visually, the baby will stare at it and then take it to his mouth. Objects placed in his hand can also be taken to his mouth. He may begin to reach out and grasp objects of interest. Now showing clear reactions, his body is developing all-round movement.

At five to six months, he can lift his head forward, can grasp his feet and hold out his arms to be lifted. He kicks strongly with alternate legs, strengthening his legs and lower back in preparation for sitting and standing.

Lying on his front, at about five months the baby arches his back and pushes up. Around the age of six months he can bear his weight on his hands with his arms straight, his spine extended and his chest and shoulders lifted from the floor (see below opposite); he can also roll from his tummy to his back. As the grasp reflex is lost and voluntary holding develops, the baby will enjoy playing and practising with objects that fit into his hand.

During these early months, because your baby is content to lie on his back, side or belly for a reasonable period of time, baby massage is made all the more easy. Once he becomes more mobile, you can move on to the following exercises for each stage of development.

Sitting

'Sit up straight', 'Sit up properly', 'Stop slouching and pay attention' are common cries the world over, as the wonderful flexibility of the baby and the postural symmetry of the infant is lost in childhood. Many of our children, who appear otherwise healthy, show signs of stiff backs, tight hips, tense shoulders and postural imbalances from an early age.

Prevention is better than cure, and when it comes to good posture it is far easier to help your child to retain it than to regain it.

As an achievement unlike anything ever witnessed in the animal kingdom, the upright posture offers major advantages, giving rapid free movement in any direction and freeing the hands to express creative and intellectual achievements. Although of an immense advantage, this posture does have one major disadvantage: it is reliable and effortless only for as long as it is properly balanced. To sit upright the baby needs to be helped, and most parents do this by pulling their babies into a sitting position by their hands (see illustration overleaf). Look what happens when you do this: there is a uniform curvature of the spine. In opposition to the direction in which he is developing, this teaches your baby to sit on his lower back, which

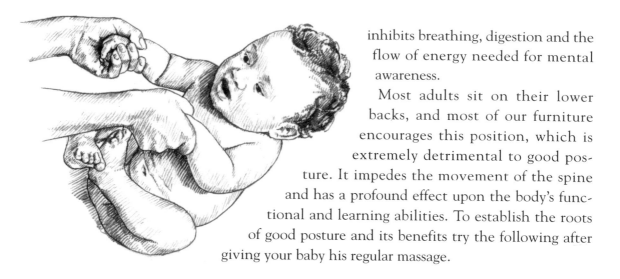

inhibits breathing, digestion and the flow of energy needed for mental awareness.

Most adults sit on their lower backs, and most of our furniture encourages this position, which is extremely detrimental to good posture. It impedes the movement of the spine and has a profound effect upon the body's functional and learning abilities. To establish the roots of good posture and its benefits try the following after giving your baby his regular massage.

Between two and three months – or once your baby has achieved a fair amount of head control – sit him with the soles of his feet together and knees open. (This position keeps his legs symmetrical with his hip joints.) Now bring your hand under your baby's arm, and supporting him from the chest, let him lean forward (this allows him to sit on the back of his legs and not the base of his spine).

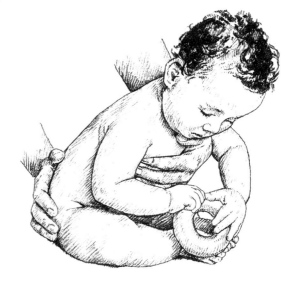

Now with your free hand, gently massage your baby's back, stroking clockwise around the upper back and then down the spine, gently pushing the base of the spine towards the floor. Repeat this several times, after every massage.

From about three to four months, sit your
baby in the same position, place a cushion
over his legs into his chest and let him lean
forward, extending his arms and hands over
the cushion. Now massage gently hand
over hand down his back from the
back of the shoulders to the base
of the spine. Again, gently push
the lower back towards the
floor to 'ground' or root your
baby. Sitting like this on the
back of his legs, your baby leaves
his spine free to move in any
direction, his chest and shoulders
open and his tummy relaxed.
Sitting, like standing, involves
balance; to be able to balance
well your baby must be securely
rooted or grounded.

When you massage your baby the next stage
is to observe him lying on his tummy to see if
he pushes up with straight arms. If he does,
you know he is ready to sit, because he is now
able to support the weight of his trunk on his
arms and hands.

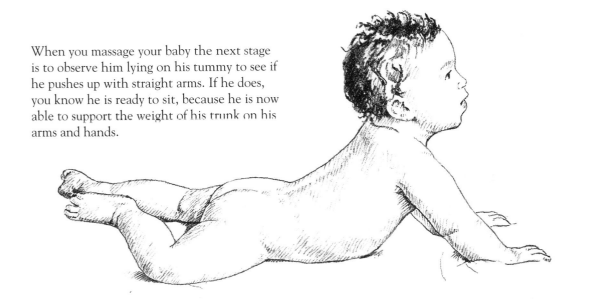

From five to six months – or when you see your baby is ready – sit him in the same position without the cushion and let him lean forward and support his weight on his arms or elbows. Don't let your baby topple forwards or sideways. Although you know he will not hurt himself, he doesn't, and assisting your child to sit in this way involves trust. If your baby falls, he will be reluctant to repeat this exercise.

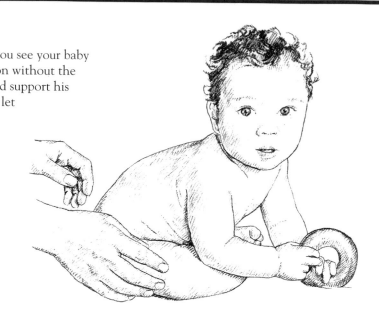

Now ground your baby by stroking hand over hand down his spine again pushing the lower back from the back of the hips gently downwards.

At about eight months, or when your baby is happy to sit unaided in this position for a few moments at a time, place your well-oiled hands on the back of his shoulders and stroke down to the base of the spine.

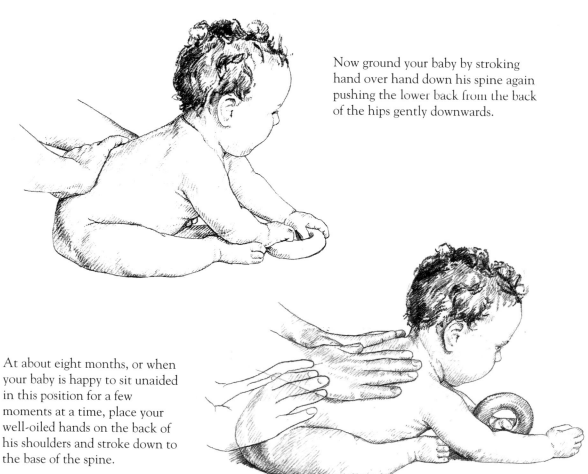

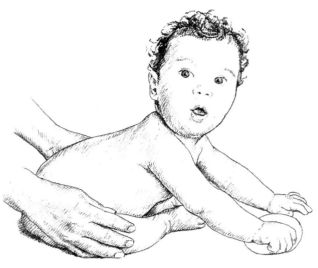

Move your hands outwards around the legs (above) and up the arms back to the shoulders (right) in one easy movement. Repeat this several times or as often as you wish. When your baby is able to support himself in this position, don't be alarmed if he leans forward and rests his head on the floor. He will not damage his hip joints – on the contrary, he is making them more flexible. You may not be able to do this movement anymore, but your baby can.

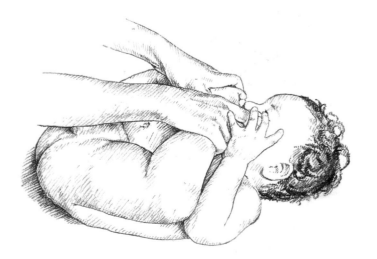

Now that your baby is able to sit unaided, the next stage – while nappy changing, after a bath, or after his routine massage – is to clap his feet together playfully and, while he is lying on his back letting his lower back lift off the floor, touch his cheeks with his feet.

Give him his feet to hold and encourage him to take them to his mouth. Massage the back of his thighs.

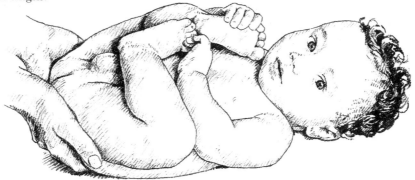

Once your baby is doing this, when sitting open his feet in line with his shoulders and place his toys between his feet to encourage him to lean forward. Massage him in this position. Go hand over hand down the back and then pull both your hands simultaneously one over each leg from the thighs to the ankles. Repeat as often as you and your baby wish.

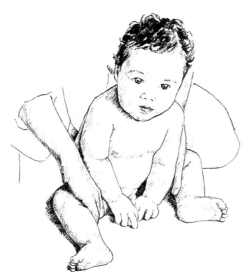

Once your baby is sitting comfortably in this position you can secure full flexibility of your baby's hip joints by opening his legs and feet a little further and massaging hand over hand down the spine and then drawing your hands over the legs from the thighs to the ankles several times.

Right When your baby is ready, let him lean forward and support his weight on his arms (see page 84).

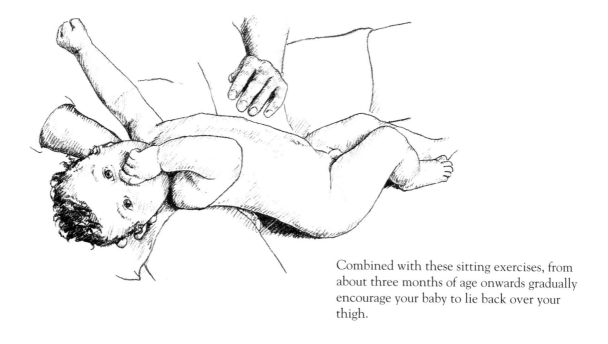

Combined with these sitting exercises, from about three months of age onwards gradually encourage your baby to lie back over your thigh.

Now, as long as he does not resist, gently ease him back slowly until the crown of his head and his feet are both touching the floor in a backbend. Now gently massage your baby's chest and belly for as long as he is content to remain in this position. This 'opens' and relaxes the front of the body. It frees the chest and tummy of tension, improves digestion, increases the breathing capacity and strengthens the back. It is also a posture that your baby will enjoy greatly if you introduce it slowly. Remember you cannot force your baby to relax. Done properly however, this is the best possible way to encourage him.

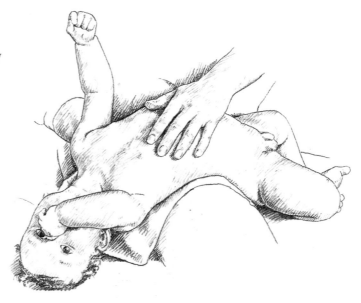

Crawling

The baby crawls in a variety of ways. At first, some babies shuffle on their bottoms. Some babies crawl backwards. Some babies crawl on their hands and knees and some on their hands and feet. Once crawling, your baby will begin to start to pull herself into a standing position holding on to furniture or whatever will sustain her weight. She will do this in her own time. Some babies crawl for days and then stand, others are content to get around by crawling for months.

To encourage your child to crawl, sit her in 'tailor pose' and put her favourite toy at her feet.

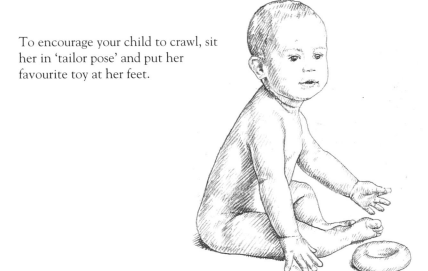

Overleaf On all fours.

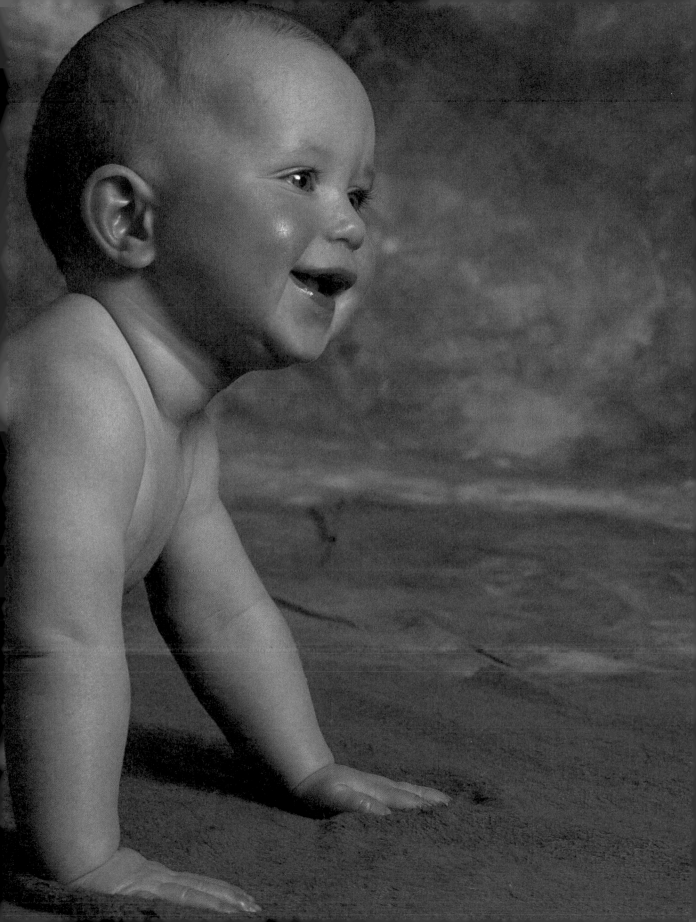

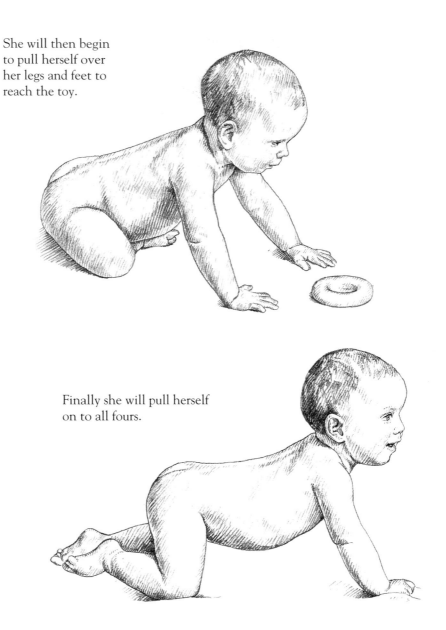

She will then begin
to pull herself over
her legs and feet to
reach the toy.

Finally she will pull herself
on to all fours.

It is important, however, to let your child enjoy and practise sitting before
moving on to crawling. Similarly, as crawling is an important phase of
development, don't hurry your baby from sitting to crawling, or from crawling to standing. Let her progress for herself, but once you see she is ready,
knowing how, you can then assist her.

Standing

When standing, babies give the appearance of being flat-footed. This is because they have a protective fatty pad under the arches of their feet. Flat feet, knock-knees and bow legs have nothing to do with letting your baby stand supported.

In the normal course of development from crawling to standing, the baby's feet are the last part of the body to develop through use. Most babies seem to enjoy being held standing and this is fine providing they are well supported. Letting your baby support his own weight, little by little for as long as this is comfortable, will help his toes to spread and his legs and back to strengthen.

Held standing, the newborn baby will not bear his body weight spontaneously on his legs, but his feet will 'walk' as they touch the floor. At around three months when this walking reflex disappears, he will begin to enjoy standing. Held standing the baby will begin to lift and turn his own head but will need to be supported from high up under his arms.

Between four and five months, held standing, the child may like to bounce and a good way to do this is to sit your baby over your thigh or your knee and let him sit and stand supported for as long as it is enjoyable. This position will encourage your baby to open his legs and feet, to provide a broad base for standing, and will also keep his feet in line with his knees. Also it will make it less tiring for you if he wants repeated practice.

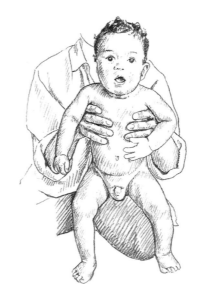

As his strength and coordination are developing you will no longer have to hold him from high up under his arms, but from around the sides of his upper chest.

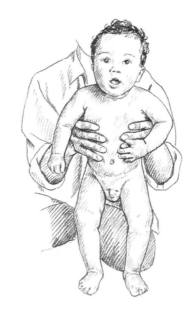

As the baby strengthens from the head and neck downwards you withdraw your support downwards, allowing the baby eventually to support his own back and then to stand unaided.

At about six to seven months the baby can stand supported and for short periods of time will bear his weight on his legs without them bending. Your support will now be from the lower chest and hips and he will still enjoy bouncing up and down.

Left Practising bouncing.

At about eight to nine months the baby can stand without bending at the knees and he may be able to pull himself up holding on to furniture, but not able to lower himself. Support can now be given holding each side of your baby's hips and from this time on it is important that you begin to ground your baby by bearing down gently pressing his 'roots', that is his legs and feet, lightly into the floor. You do this by holding each side of the hips and just resting the weight of your hands there. Don't pull your baby down – just the weight of your hands is all that is needed to give your child strong roots.

Balance depends upon security, and the more secure your baby is through his roots (his legs and feet) the stronger his posture will be. Your baby will also want to run before he can stand; bearing down gently in this way will ground him and help him consolidate his current position to get the feel of standing properly first.

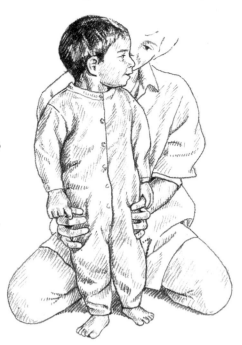

Between nine and ten months the baby will pull himself into a standing position from sitting and let himself down with a bump; between ten and eleven months he will stand holding on to furniture and lift and lower his feet. By twelve months the child may stand unaided briefly, stand and walk sideways holding on to reliable furniture, or walk with support, or may walk alone.

The average age at which a child walks without support is about thirteen months, and at this age he will also stand unaided briefly. When walking his legs and feet will be apart to give a broad base for balance but he may fall repeatedly. He will also begin to crawl upstairs; as soon as he begins to do this it is important that you show him how to crawl downstairs by coming down backwards.

At about fifteen months he can go from sitting to standing unaided, will walk unevenly, letting himself down backwards with a bump or falling forwards on to his hands and then sitting backwards. He finds it difficult to stop and to negotiate corners. He may kneel unaided and stoop to pick up objects from the floor, and may enjoy pushing a large wheeled toy on level ground. Usually he will sit in a chair by facing it, climbing on to it, standing on it, turning around and sitting down.

The ages at which children sit, crawl, stand and walk vary enormously and it is of great benefit to the development of the child's nervous system as a whole that they are not hurried, but rather allowed to proceed at their own pace.

Aids for mobility

There is an ever-increasing number of innovative toys on the market for babies and toddlers, but it is worth bearing in mind that some are more suitable than others for each stage of development. For example, babies really seem to enjoy baby bouncers, and these seem fine for short amounts of time. However, the emphasis with a baby bouncer is to lift the baby up at a time when they really need to be grounded.

Baby bouncers

If your baby has a bouncer, once she is able to sit unsupported rather than encouraging her to stand up on her toes, sit her in her baby bouncer with her feet on the floor and her knees bent in the same way as you would sit her astride your thigh.

Letting your baby bounce up and down without her feet actually fully leaving the ground – for short periods of time – eliminates any risk of her compressing her joints and will help her strengthen her legs for standing.

Climbing frames

A climbing frame, or something similar, which the baby can reach and is secure enough to support her weight as she pulls herself up into a standing position and lets herself down again gently, is a good aid to standing from squatting. This is an excellent tool to aid this practice as well as providing a framework to 'walk' around.

Push carts

A good push cart, either weighted or with adjustable wheels, is one that will not 'run away' with the child when she stands and pushes it. Unlike a baby walker, once the baby is standing it will help her to walk slowly and in the right direction.

Once walking, toddlers and infants seem to have great fun with four-wheelers that they can sit astride, steer, and propel forward with their legs and feet.

Mobility and Independence

For your child mobility opens up new horizons and offers many exciting opportunities for discovery and development. Up until now it has always been that you walk away from your baby, as a major step towards independence; now for the first time, mobility allows your baby to leave *you*.

In many traditional societies, like the Ibo and Onitsha of West Africa and the Australian Aboriginals, this 'natural break' is cultivated, and the child receives great praise for his physical prowess, and much encouragement to run, jump, roll, swing, climb and so on. This attitude seems to recognise the relationship between self-confidence and independence, as it encourages the child to trust more in his own skills and abilities and feel at home in his own environment, whatever his allotted space may be.

Young children love to explore their physical potential and they develop self-reliance with spirit and determination. Now no longer content to remain in any one position, the child will not be 'pinned down' for massage – or anything else – but will want to explore and pursue movement and will strengthen rapidly as he lifts and carries his ever-increasing body weight from place to place.

A sound mind dwells in a sound body

... do not develop one physical attribute

at the expense of another.

HIPPOCRATES (460–377BC)

Flexibility and health

Strength and suppleness are essential components of health and fitness, and vital ingredients to all forms of dance, sports, games and other physical activities. From the 1930s to the 1950s, flexibility exercise formulated from the German and Swedish gymnastics of Frederick Jann and Per Ling was mandatory to the curriculum of all schools throughout the United Kingdom. Today its demise is reflected in the poor level of flexibility enjoyed by most children, and the idolising of aggressive strength – a current trend which has a negative affect upon posture and personality.

Inflexibility is a subtle disorder which begins in childhood as the baby strengthens in response to gravity. Like all weightlifting, if not combined with expansive movement, the process of strengthening diminishes flexibility. As an insidious part of the ageing process, inflexibility remains hidden, but accumulates with time to reveal itself as stiffness in the muscles and joints in later childhood, or as one of a variety of associated disorders that affect the majority of adults.

If any of the body's organs – the heart, lungs, liver or spleen – were not functioning properly, they would receive immediate attention. The body's muscles and joints are organs of sensation and movement, the very essence of life and they are designed for a specific range of mobility. If they cannot fulfil this range then they are not functioning healthily, and as such they should be given at least the same attention as the inner organs that support their activities. Having got this far and already encouraged your baby to establish a high degree of muscular relaxation, a little playful attention given now will ensure the flexibility of all his major joints while his body strengthens and help him to avoid some of the problems mentioned above.

The more interaction between parent and child, the better. And because your child no longer remains still to be massaged, it does not mean that you cannot continue to develop the kind of relationship that massage facilitated. In fact, by taking it a step further, you can continue to encourage:

- trust and confidence in your relationship;
- an even development of muscular strength and suppleness;
- good posture with a wide range of versatile movements;
- the self-confidence that comes with strength and flexibility.

It is far easier to retain flexibility than it is to regain it. And to meet this requirement, you can utilise your child's love of movement, engaging him in a few easy and effective swings and stretches that maintain his flexibility as he rapidly strengthens.

Although these movements are therapeutic, like massage they demand muscular relaxation and therefore the cooperation of your baby. Done *with* a baby and not *to* a baby, these simple movements are enjoyable, so if your baby objects take it as an indication that you are either engaging her in the wrong way or at the wrong time. Perseverance brings success, but reassess how and when you do the movements. Practised with lots of hugs and kisses for rewards and a few favourite nursery rhymes, they become games, and like baby massage can give you the opportunity of pleasurable and highly therapeutic one-to-one interludes of play with your child.

Introduce these games individually, and as your baby anticipates and enjoys each one, practise them as two separate five-minute routines, one for the legs and one for the body.

The legs

TAILOR POSE SWING

Once your baby can sit securely without your support, you can engage your child in this game to maintain flexibility of his hip joints. This game can be played up to two or three years of age or longer if you can comfortably lift and swing your child without too much effort.

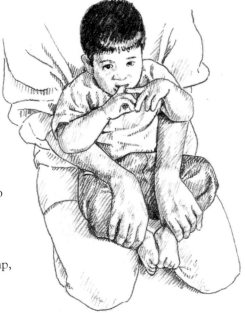

Sit on your feet with your baby on your lap, sitting feet together with his knees open. Bring your arms under his and hold him from the ankles.

Now make a harness with your forearms and thumbs and pick your baby up by his ankles, letting him lean slightly forward. Now swing him gently from side to side.

Having practised tailor pose swing and feeling comfortable with it, swing your baby gently from side to side and bounce him gently to encourage him to drop his chest forward on to his feet.

Now sit your baby on the floor. See how he sits on the backs of his legs, leaving his spine completely free.

Until you feel completely confident with this exercise, when you swing your child do it gently and keep him very close to the ground. Once you have practised the above a few times, add the following sequence.

SINGING SIDESPLITS

Following tailor pose swing, sit your baby in front of you. Use a favourite nursery rhyme and part the legs in rhythm, opening and closing them one leg at a time (leaving one leg in tailor pose as you open the other leg sideways). Repeat for both legs a few times.

Open and close both legs together from tailor pose to sidesplits.

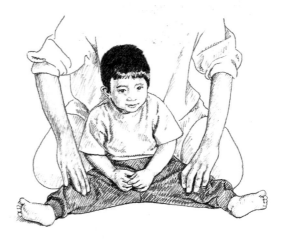

Keeping in rhythm with the nursery rhyme and with both legs in sidesplits, apply light percussion to the inside thighs, patting them very quickly with the palms of your hands.

This encourages the inside thigh (adductor) muscles to relax while the sound will engage your baby's attention. The inside thighs are among the first of the muscle groups that tighten once your baby is walking; they tighten for the purpose of keeping the legs together for standing, walking and running. Stiffness in these muscles inhibits good posture by making the hip joints inflexible. This affects both the ease with which the body sits, stands and moves, and the body's range of movement, sitting or standing.

Right *Sitting in sidesplits.*

Once your baby begins to crawl, add the following exercise.

PAT-A-CHEEK

Sitting on your feet, with your baby sitting in tailor pose in front of you, give your baby a tailor pose swing and then sit him on your lap.

Now lean back and 'clap' your baby's feet to his face. To make this enjoyable, tap his cheeks with his feet, in rhythm to 'Pat-a-Cake' (or any other favourite nursery rhyme). Do this for about half a minute.

You can also do this exercise by encouraging your baby to kiss his toes when he is lying on the floor, when nappy changing or drying him after his bath. This keeps the backs of the legs supple as they strengthen.

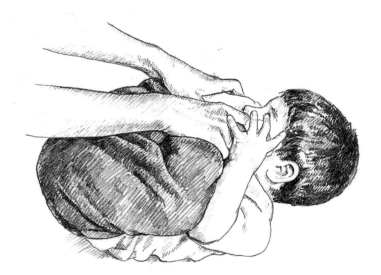

Once you have made this enjoyable, complete the
routine with the following.

Give your baby a tailor pose
swing, then, leaning back,
take his feet to his cheeks.
Now, still leaning
back, open his
legs and feet and
rock him gently
from side to side
a few times.

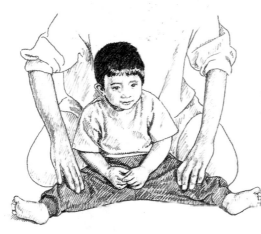

Next sit your baby on the
floor, legs and feet apart, and
apply light percussion.

Maintaining the flexibility of your baby's hips and legs is as important to
learning as it is to posture and movement. When a child sits on the backs of
their legs, their mental faculties are clearer and more alert; unhampered by
inner sensations of discomfort, the child is more aware and therefore more
able to digest information from their external environment. Walk into any
infant or junior classroom: those children with good posture will be the ones
with the longest span of attention.

The body

Once your baby is crawling and standing, with lots of hugs and kisses you can engage her in some simple games to maintain the flexibility of her spine. Bending backwards is a movement children make and enjoy from a very early age. Maintaining this movement keeps the front of the body, the belly, chest and shoulders open and relaxed, and encourages the back to strengthen. This is of great importance to good posture.

As you do the backbends, 'bounce' your baby very, very gently. If you do this right you will find your baby's subtle rhythm and she will open and relax.

BACKBENDS

Sitting on your feet with your baby sitting belly to belly, her legs and feet open around your waist, with one hand supporting the back of your baby's head and the other the upper-back across her shoulder blades, lean your baby backwards.

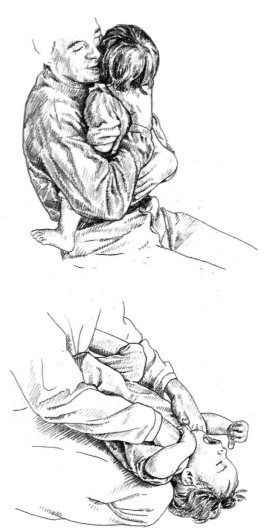

As her head goes back, push her chest gently forward. Bounce her very gently to send a gentle wave along her spine.

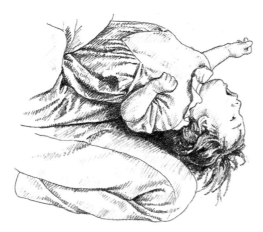

Now lower her back over your knees. Place your hands over her shoulders with your hands **inside her arms**.

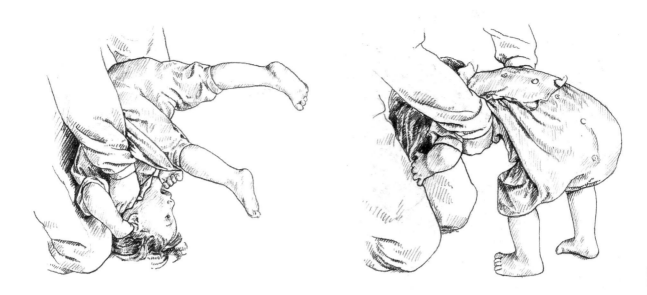

Now stand up on your knees, taking care that her legs are free to backward roll through your arms.

Finally, hold her supported standing.

Your baby will enjoy this backward roll and once you are relaxed and fluid with it she will anticipate it and will also greatly enjoy the feeling of you opening her chest before you lay her on to your knees.

Once you are confident with the above, try the following.

Standing up, or standing on your knees, open your baby's legs around your waist and hug them to the sides of your body with your elbows. Now the same as before, let your baby take her head backwards as you push her chest forwards, your hands on her shoulder blades. Again, bounce her very, very gently a few times and send a gentle wave along her spine.

Now, holding her legs securely with your elbows and her chest with your hands, lower her head first towards the floor.

Transfer your hands one at a time to hold your baby by her ankles and lower her so that her hands just touch the floor. Now swing her very gently from side to side before lowering her.

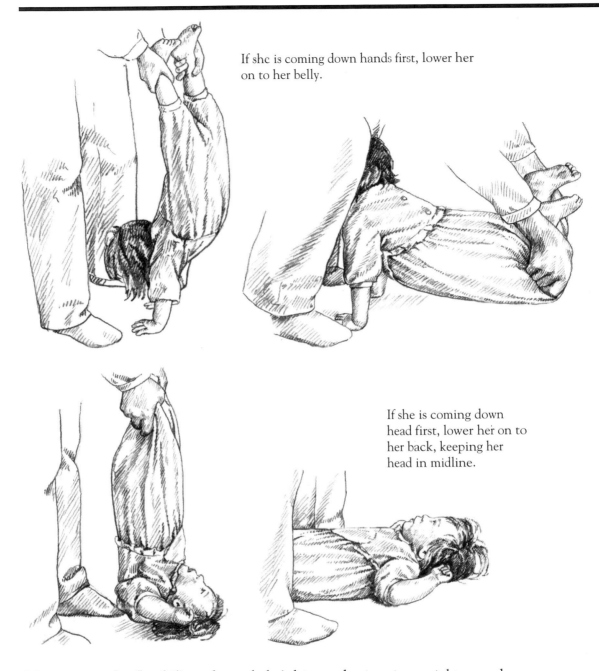

If she is coming down hands first, lower her on to her belly.

If she is coming down head first, lower her on to her back, keeping her head in midline.

Maintaining the flexibility of your baby's hips and spine, is crucial to good posture, both sitting and standing. It encourages good breathing and digestive rhythms and a balanced relationship with gravity that will not impose undue stress on the child's muscles and joints. Children who have developed strength and flexibility evenly are the ones who play sports and games with far less risk of injury. Because of their wider range of movement and the confidence that comes with a fit body, they are also far more likely to excel in them.

CHAPTER FOUR

A Healing Touch

Being held, touched and caressed is like food to the baby, food as necessary as minerals, vitamins and proteins.

FREDERICK LEBOYER
Loving Hands

Special Care

Massage has a valuable part to play in caring for babies with special needs. There are only a few impairments that prohibit touching and stroking. Chronic skin conditions and medical procedures or conditions which render the baby inaccessible or hypersensitive to touch are the most obvious. Whatever the situation, however, it is important that you talk with a sympathetic consultant to know what you can do for your child, and how best to integrate your approach with your baby's treatment.

Touching, holding and massaging your baby cannot hurt her – on the contrary a loving touch will help her to thrive. Once possible, introduce massage slowly in the ways suggested earlier in the book, and the massage routine itself should give you a starting point which you can develop to suit your baby's needs.

Babies who remain for long periods of time in incubators or intensive care can begin to associate touch with medical procedures, and may cry when being handled. A consultant who recognises the loneliness of an incubator may encourage you to hold your baby's hand, and wherever and whenever possible to lay warm, relaxed hands on your baby, stroke and possibly nappy-change your baby, and develop as much skin-to-skin contact as possible.

Sometimes the baby's hands and feet are punctured by drips, drains and transfusions. When the wounds have healed, holding the baby's hands and forearms in your relaxed hands, and then gently massaging them between your palms, will restore relaxation and renew the warmth of circulation. The same approach can be applied to your baby's feet and legs.

Opiates like morphine are given routinely to premature babies who show signs of acute distress, and phenobarbitone is sometimes given to babies diagnosed as epileptic. Massage can be a useful antidote to ease both the withdrawal of the comfort provided by the treatment and the baby's return from any dependence on it.

The premature baby

Given first-rate neonatal care, the survival rate for babies born at twenty-three weeks is, at best, twenty per cent and approximately one third of these will suffer no long-term effects; for those born at twenty-four weeks the survival rate almost doubles to somewhere around thirty-five per cent. This marked increase in survival is due to advances in the quality and sophistication of the care provided, and fundamental physiological developments present at twenty-four weeks, which determine the baby's potential to survive independently.

Through the umbilical connection with the placenta, the baby receives oxygenated blood nutrients and minerals; between twenty-four and twenty-eight weeks babies develop pockets in the recesses of their lungs which provide a site for oxygenation. Without these air sacs, even if the lungs are ventilated, oxygenation cannot take place – and consequently the baby cannot survive.

For those babies who can survive, some weighing less than a two-pound bag of sugar, doctors try to recreate the kind of conditions furnished by the womb. Because handling can be stressful, feeding is done intravenously, and monitors are used constantly to observe survival systems like the heart beat, blood pressure and body temperature within the sterile environments of an incubator kept at precisely 37.4°C.

Although handling can be stressful for the very premature baby, an incubator can be lonely. Perhaps more than at any other period in life, this is a time for mindfulness – for soft sounds, shaded light and touching or holding with warm relaxed hands. Try not to over-stimulate and bombard the baby's senses with sound, sight and touch, and be aware of any perfume or aromas that the baby may find distressing.

As previously mentioned, research shows that touching stimulates the peripheral and autonomic nervous systems and the body's major organs. Start by avoiding the monitors and supports, just placing your warm, relaxed hands on the accessible parts of your baby's body. Feel your baby with the palms of your hands and just breathe and relax. Don't look for feedback, this will come in time – at this stage your baby needs the reassurance of a loving presence. Maintain this kind of contact daily, as often as you can, gradually increasing the duration of touching from moments to minutes as you feel it is appropriate.

As and when holding becomes possible, take your time and remember to hold your baby in relaxed hands. Take her in the palms of your hands by using them and by feeling with them. Holding and the laying on of hands can be a rewarding experience for you and your baby, and once you are able you can introduce massage. Because your baby is 'pre-term' she is likely to feel even more vulnerable than a full-term baby; so bear this in mind, and obviously do not insist that she straightens her limbs, which are likely to remain folded for a while for self-protection. And, where possible, use your whole hand when stroking – a warm, relaxed hand will convey trust and security.

Caesarean section

The delivery of a child by cutting through the walls of the abdomen was given the name Caesarean after Julius Caesar, who was born in the same manner. Babies born by Caesarean section miss the stimulation of protract-ed contractions that accompanies a normal birth. Other mammals who tend to have multiple births and consequently rapid deliveries which similarly fail to confer this kind of stimulation, like cats and dogs, give their newborn a good licking. This is known to have a profound effect upon the function-ing of their young's genito-urinary system. For those babies delivered by Caesarean section, cutaneous stimulation of the kind conferred by oiling, stroking and massage both stimulates the principal systems of survival and gives the mother and child an opportunity to 'get in touch', usually impracticable at birth because of the medical attention needed by the mother.

For premature babies, babies born by Caesarean section, and those babies removed from their mothers for the time immediately following their birth, a little extra care is sometimes needed to allay their anxieties. A very premature baby, or one needing medical attention at birth, may need a lot more reassurance. The holding position shown on page 115 can be a very effective way to calm a fractious or anxious baby. If your baby, however, remains fractious, you can also try bathing with him and feeding him in the bath. Add a tablespoon of olive oil to the bath water and stroke him gently while he feeds.

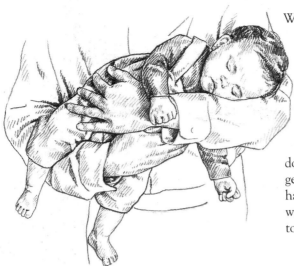

When all else seems to fail to pacify your baby, cradle his head and neck in the crook of your **left** arm and let him wrap his arms and legs around your arms facing outwards. Generally walking him in this position will, more often than not, calm him. If it doesn't, try patting his tummy gently but quickly with your right hand or gently massaging it while walking and talking to him in low tones.

Massage for babies with physical impairments

Babies with conditions such as cerebral palsy and quadriplegia can also benefit from being massaged. Muscle tone can be influenced, circulation stimulated and relief given from the effects of acute wind and constipation, all of which are aggravated by the child's lack of mobility. Establishing a basic massage routine will give you the feel of your baby and the confidence needed to work more closely with your child's physiotherapist. It will allow you to integrate their techniques with some that you know your baby enjoys the most, as well as giving you the opportunity to participate more in your baby's treatment. It will also give you the opportunity to 'treat' your baby daily. The main advantage is that it will allow you to treat your baby with a parent's love more frequently, at the most appropriate time, rather than your baby having to receive treatment – whether they are on for it or not – on a more occasional basis.

Babies with visual impairment may also benefit greatly from massage. The impairment of one sense often impels the development of another. This is especially so with a visual impairment, whereby the child must use his tactile senses to define his world and give form and substance to the things which surround him.

Vocalising your actions, and describing the different parts of the body as you massage them, is of great value to the child in establishing a body image.

When appropriate, the techniques used to encourage sitting, crawling and standing will also be of value, but you will need to put your child 'in touch' with the objects used to assist crawling and standing.

Babies with an auditory impairment also need to be spoken to, and to receive visual as well as tactile cues of reassurance. Talk to your baby and imitate his sounds as you would normally. Describe what you are doing and punctuate your massage with expressions of affection like clapping your baby's feet together, kissing them, blowing on them and giving him a few light strokes down the front of his body from his shoulders to his feet.

Babies with an auditory or visual impairment may not enjoy lying on their bellies. If this is the case, place a cushion under your baby's chest so that his legs and belly remain on the floor while his chest and head are slightly elevated. Begin your back massage with very light percussion, patting around the back of the chest and shoulders with cupped hands.

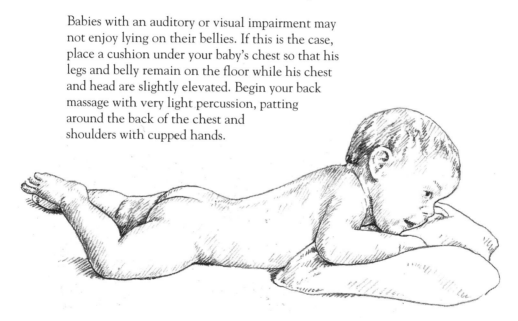

Above all, massaging your baby is meant to be a pleasurable experience for you both. Although highly therapeutic, massage is not a treatment; rather it is something you do with – not to – your baby. Introduce massage slowly, and if your baby gets upset, stop and return to it when he is more receptive. Most babies will respond immediately; if not, after at most three or four sessions, he will begin to anticipate and enjoy it. Perseverance brings success, and introducing massage is a very special way to care for your baby.

Common Childhood Ailments

Massage can also help you to cope with some of the more everyday problems of childhood. You can alleviate some of the discomfort caused by wind, constipation and colic, as well as help relieve congestion and thus encourage your baby to get a better night's sleep.

Digestion and relaxation

Some doctors agree that mothers often ascribe their baby's distress to disorders of the digestive system, namely wind or colic. They say the need to be held, nurtured and played with, and hunger, teething and sometimes even illness are overlooked because wind and colic are convenient explanations. Most mothers, however, agree that as a result of their babies' physical immaturity they do experience wind and sometimes colic, and that traditional methods of winding their babies bring relief.

Wind

Adults and children alike ingest air along with their intake of solids and liquids, and it is quite normal for there to be air in the stomach and intestines. However, the very young child may ingest an uncomfortable amount of air into the stomach while feeding and, because of the immaturity of the baby's digestive system, air in the intestines can sometimes result in an uncomfortable pocket of gas.

Correct positioning of your baby during and after feeding can help prevent excessive wind and provide relief. If your child is slouched or horizontal

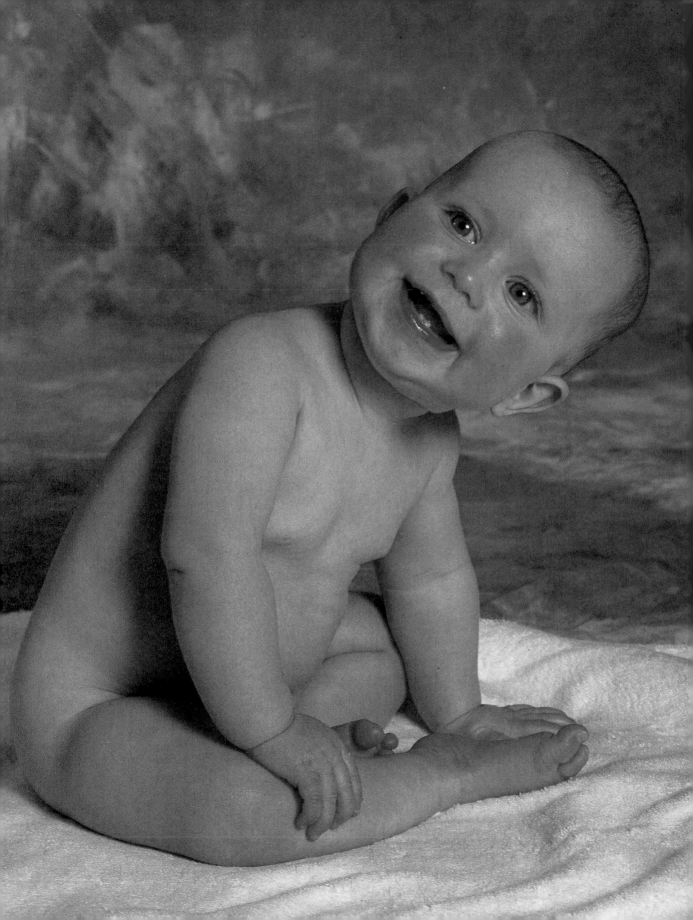

while feeding, air can accumulate in the stomach until it becomes considerably distended. The subsequent release of air tends to cause milk to be brought up. Keeping your baby's back reasonably straight during feeding, with the lower back supported upright, will help her to expel excessive air readily.

After a feed you can help your baby to release 'wind' as follows. Sitting with your child on your knees, leaning forward supported by one of your hands across the upper chest, stroke her back from the base of the spine, upwards only. Then pat gently between her shoulder blades.

This can also be done with your baby lying across one shoulder. Some parents find this position more comfortable and more effective.

If your baby lies on her side, when you lay her down after a feed it is best to place her on her right side. If the child is placed on her left side any air that may be in the stomach tends to pass into the intestine, which can cause discomfort.

If your baby suffers from wind, colic or constipation, check with your doctor first to ensure that she is not ill or allergic to something in her or your own diet if you are breastfeeding. Also check that she is not suffering from a lack of fluid as sometimes happens when a baby starts on solids.

Left Happy, healthy and relaxed!

If your baby is distressed and on and off the breast at a regular time in the evening or late afternoon, make sure that you are taking adequate nourishment and the time to digest it properly. Don't ignore your own hunger pangs, eat regularly and give yourself time to enjoy it.

Wind, colic and constipation can be alleviated through the regular practice of the following techniques. Holding your baby in the position shown on page 115 while patting and massaging her tummy can relieve the symptoms when they are acute. Regularly massaging your baby, giving extra attention to the tummy, will also help but not when your baby is in distress. Lying your baby on her tummy will also help to stretch and relax this area, but do not do this immediately after a feed as the advice given is that babies should not sleep in this position. Regular massage before bedtime using a few drops of the essential oil of camomile well diluted in your base oil can also bring a measure of relief. If you use lots of oil and wipe your baby 'dry' with a soft, warm towel this can substitute for a bath and encourage her to relax more.

Breathing

Of all things necessary to life, to maintain and improve the healthy functioning and development of the body, oxygen is perhaps the most important. 'To breathe little is to feel little', 'Inhibited breathing results in anxiety … apathy … loss of self-control … loss of concentration'. These are some of the conclusions of physical therapists and doctors, and modern medicine now recognises physiotherapy as an invaluable part of the treatment of asthma and related disorders.

You will see that your child breathes with his lower chest and abdomen, which expand and contract in unison. This kind of breathing – abdominal breathing – is found only in children, good athletes, and healthy, relaxed adults. It allows the base of the lungs, the diaphragm, to descend into the abdomen. This has two major advantages as far as the healthy functioning of the body is concerned: firstly, it increases the volume of oxygen inhaled and, secondly, it massages the belly. With every inhalation the diaphragm descends, pushing the belly outwards as it gently presses upon its contents. With each exhalation the diaphragm rises and as it does so creates a vacuum that draws the belly and its contents inwards. Belly breathing greatly relaxes the internal organs and stimulates their function. This 'gentle massage' takes place over 15,000 times every twenty-four hours.

Breathing and flexibility

The lungs are passive containers that are pulled into movement with the action of the rib-cage. Their breathing capacity is dependent on the flexibility of the chest and on good posture, a straight back and open shoulders. When combined with a relaxed abdomen, this gives the maximum amount of oxygen for the least amount of effort.

All babies breathe through their nostrils. Therefore, when the nostrils are congested minor respiratory disorders such as coughs and colds can prove a greater source of discomfort at night, as they interfere with the child's natural rhythm of respiration and disturb her sleep.

With the change from wakefulness to sleep the body relaxes and the breathing rhythm becomes deeper and slower. If at this time the baby's breathing is obstructed through her nostrils, the child usually awakens with a start as she breathes in through her mouth, and this can make her irritable and unhappy.

Relieving congestion

A chest and back massage given just before bedtime with a blend of lavender, myrrh or frankincense and base massage oil (see page 31) can be combined with the technique overleaf to help relieve congestion and bring relief plus a good night's sleep.

The massage techniques given to relax the chest and belly, together with exercises for the chest and abdomen (for the older child), will help promote and maintain a regular rhythm of deep, relaxed breathing.

If your baby is heavily congested also place her in a more upright position when sleeping. Never let your baby sleep on pillows to raise her head but rather raise the head of her cot on books or something similar. A few drops of essential oil of lavender, frankincense or myrrh, used as directed in a bath or base massage oil, or two drops neat on the front of your baby's night clothes can also bring relief.

N.B. IF YOUR BABY IS POORLY ALWAYS SEEK PROFESSIONAL ADVICE. THESE TECHNIQUES ARE NOT MEANT TO SUBSTITUTE FOR PROFESSIONAL DIAGNOSIS AND CARE.

RELIEVING CONGESTION

With your baby lying back supported upon your thighs, trace the outline of her cheekbones from the sides of her nose, pressing gently downwards and outwards with your index fingers. This helps to relieve congestion by opening the nostrils. (Try this on yourself first to make sure you have the correct technique.)

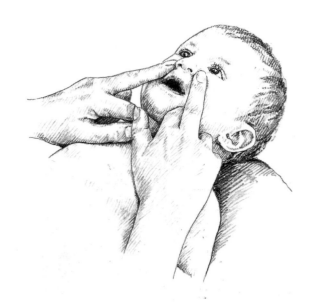

To relieve the chest, lay your baby over your thighs with her head and trunk leaning backwards over your knees and pat the centre and sides of the chest with cupped hands.

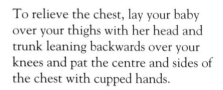

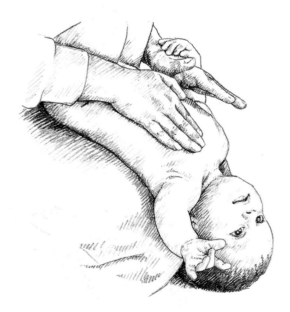

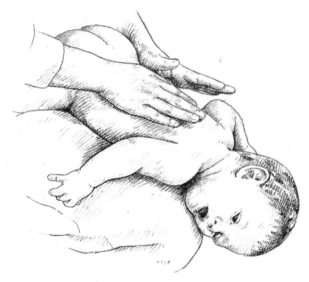

Now turn your baby on to her belly and repeat across the upper back. The patting and suction of cupped hands helps to loosen the mucus. If congestion is heavy, vomiting can occur. This muscular activity expels the mucus by compressing the lungs and bronchial tubes.

RECOMMENDED READING

Balaskas, Janet and Gordon, Yehudi, *The Encyclopaedia of Pregnancy and Birth*, Macdonald Orbis

Ferber, Dr Richard, *Solve Your Chid's Sleep Problems*, Dorling Kindersley

Goldsmith, Judith, *Childbirth Wisdom*, East West Natural Health Books, US

Jackson, Deborah, *Three in a Bed*, Bloomsbury

Leach, Penelope, *Children First*, Penguin

Litt, Jerome Z, *Your Skin and How to Live in It*, Ballantine, US (o.p.)

Liedloff, Jean, *The Continuum Concept*, Penguin Books

Miller, Alice, *The Drama of Being a Child*, Virago

Montagu, Ashley, *Touching: The Human Significance of Skin*, Harper & Row

Pearce, Joseph Chilton, *Magical Child*, Granada Publishing (o.p.)

Ryman, Danièle, *Aromatherapy: The Encyclopaedia of Plants and Oils and How They Help You*, Piatkus Books

Winnicott, D.W., *The Child, the Family and the Outside World*, Penguin

USEFUL ADDRESSES

If you would like to find out about baby massage classes in your area or receive information about postnatal exercise, send a stamped, addressed envelope to the following address:

Peter Walker
PO Box 8293
London W9 2WZ

Copies of Peter Walker's video *Loving Baby Massage* are also available from this address priced £11.99, (including posting and package UK only). Cheques or postal orders should be made payable to East Atlantic Video.

Other useful addresses in the UK include:

The Active Birth Centre
25 Bickerton Road
London N19 5JT
Tel: 0171-561 9006
For preparation and education for child-birth, UK teachers' list available (please send a stamped, addressed envelope)

Gingerbread
49 Wellington Street
London WC2E 7BN
Tel: 0171-240 0953
For a national network of local groups for single parents

The Health Visitors' Association
50 Southwark Street
London SE1 1NW

Your local health visitor can be con-tacted through your GP's surgery, local health centre or clinic

Irish Childbirth Trust
5 Grange Manor Road
Rathfarnham
Dublin 16
Tel: 353 1 493 5969
For mother-to-mother support, educa-tion for parenthood, antenatal classes, postnatal and breastfeeding support

La Leche League of Great Britain
27 Old Gloucester Street
London WC1N 3XX
Tel: 0171-242 1278
For breastfeeding counsellors

National Childbirth Trust
Alexandra House
Oldham Terrace
London W3 6NH
Tel: 0181-992 8637
For childbirth educators

National Council for One Parent
Families
255 Kentish Town Road

London NW5 2LX
Tel: 0171-267 1361
*For free publications and information
on housing, maintenance, grants, benefits, divorce etc*

Parentline
Tel: 01702 559900
*National network of helplines for par-
ents under stress*

Useful addresses worldwide:

AUSTRALIA

For active birth teachers:

Adelaide Active Birth Centre (Julie
Pearse)
24 Dalton Avenue
Aldgate, Adelaide 5154

Associates in Childbirth Education
(Andrea Robertson)
P O Box 366
Camperdown, NSW 2050

Centre of Awareness (Leena Clarke)
294 Smith Street
Collingwood 3066
Melbourne, Victoria

CANADA

Childcare Resources and Research
455 Spadina Avenue
Toronto
Ontario M5S 2G8
Tel: (416) 978 6895
For information on daycare

La Leche League of Canada
P O Box 29
Chesterville
Ontario K0C 1H0
Tel: (613) 448 1842

NEW ZEALAND

New Zealand College of Midwives
(INC)
Ground floor McCann–Erickson House
906-908 Colombo Street
PO Box 21-106
Christchurch
Tel: (03) 3772 732

USA

International Childbirth Education
Association
P O Box 20048
Minneapolis
MN 55402
Tel: (612) 854 8660
For active birth information

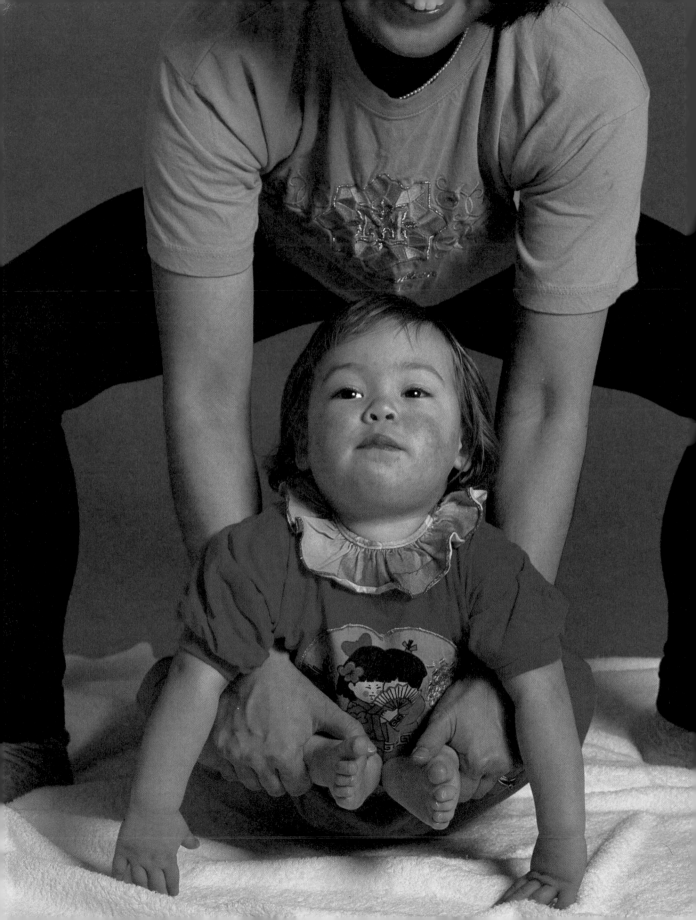

INDEX

Left Practising tailor pose swing (see page 100).